MW01290589

# Dark Psychology and Manipulation

*For a Better Life: The Ultimate*

*Guide to Learning the Art of*

*Persuasion, Emotional Influence,*

*NLP Secrets, Hypnosis, Body*

*Language, and Mind Control*

*Techniques*

**PUBLISHED BY: Brandon Goleman**

## © Copyright 2019 - All rights reserved.

# Table of Contents

## Chapter 4: Dark Persuasion Methods

### Neuro-Linguistic Programming and Non-verbal Communication

What Is NLP?

Verbal and Non-verbal Communication

How does NLP work?

Is NLP Effective?

### Hypnosis

What is Hypnosis?

What Are the Uses of Hypnosis?

Myths About Hypnosis

Facts About Hypnosis

### Hypnotherapy

What Happens During Hypnotherapy?

Is Hypnotherapy Effective?

Drawbacks of Hypnotherapy

### Brainwashing

What is Brainwashing?

The History of Brainwashing

Brainwashing Today

# Introduction

The pace of change in the world today is occurring at the speed of a microprocessor. Never in human history have we undergone the kinds of revolutionary changes in communication, travel, and business that we have all witnessed in just a few short years.

Despite all the rapid modernization and digitization, people are still people. Though many of these abrupt changes have disputed our familiar routines and customs, we still process information and seek many of the same goals in our personal and professional lives that we always have. And as in the past, we are still plagued by certain elements of the population who engage in harmful and destructive behavior.

This propensity for dark psychology lies within each of us, and as the world changes with the advent of digital technology, we must also adapt our responses to these deviant social behaviors.

*Dark Psychology and Manipulation - For a Better Life: The Ultimate Guide to Learning the Art of Persuasion, Emotional Influence, NLP Secrets, Hypnosis, Body Language, and Mind Control Techniques* provides readers with an overview of what clinical psychologists have learned about deviant personalities and how they have learned to adapt in the new tech-heavy environment that seems to permeate everything these days.

This book will give readers the essential information they need not only to resist and protect themselves from the impositions of emotional and social predators, but also how to develop a high degree of emotional intelligence that will allow them to succeed in the modern workplace and get the best out of the self-improvement programs that can help you make the techniques of emotional predators work for you, not against you.

# Chapter 1:

# Delving into Dark Psychology

Dark psychology may conjure up thoughts of intrigue and even romance. Films and television productions like *Dexter*, *GoodFellas*, *CSI*, and *Criminal Minds* have popularized notions of serial killers and "tough but fair" business moguls who hold the city in a tight grip of brutality that is necessary for the greater prosperity and security of everyone.

The truth is, dark psychology is more than just a term in popular culture that describes the alluring, exciting, and adventurous lifestyles of rock stars, international financiers, and crime experts. Popular culture has developed an entire vocabulary to describe the people in our lives who may be displaying alarmingly high levels of predatory behavior. Whole genres of sitcoms and films depict the comic adventures of otherwise happy and well-adjusted young people trapped in toxic relationships.

We have learned to accept to an uncomfortable degree the increasingly common presence of predatory and abusive personality types in our daily lives. So, we often overlook or may be unaware that dark psychology has its roots in serious clinical psychology and has been a subject of scientific inquiry for centuries. This chapter will explore some of the basic terminology and historical and practical contexts in which this aspect of human relationships still maintains relevant.

## Theoretical Overview

According to Dr. Michael Nuccitelli, Psy.D., dark psychology can be defined as follows:

> *Dark psychology is both a human consciousness construct and study of the human condition as it relates to the psychological nature of people to prey upon others motivated by psychopathic, deviant, or*

*psychopathological criminal drives that lack purpose and general assumptions of instinctual drives, evolutionary biology, and social sciences theory. All of humanity has the potentiality to victimize humans and other living creatures. While many restrain or sublimate this tendency, some act upon these impulses. Dark psychology explores criminal, deviant, and cybercriminal minds* (Nuccitelli, 2006).

Thus, dark psychology explores the psychological state of people who exhibit a tendency toward predatory behavior.

The work of Dr. Nuccitelli is based upon work completed by Dr. Alfred Adler. At the beginning of the 20th century, Dr. Adler, a medical doctor, psychologist, philosopher, and contemporary of Dr. Carl Jung and Dr. Sigmund Freud, compiled a volume of work exploring many behavioral and psychological theories in an effort to explain why some people are prone to commit acts of predatory violence and abuse. From the perspective of Dr. Adler, all human behavior is motivated by a rational purpose. Thus, for Adler, neither good behavior nor bad behavior can be attributed to the basic, fundamental character of the person; instead, all behavior can only be explained by examining the motivations and goals of the person.

For example, a benevolent or kind person behaves in such a manner, not because he or she is a fundamentally kind or caring person, but because he or she has been taught since childhood that kind, caring, and contributory behavior is more likely to result in acceptance by social groups. Further, acceptance into social groups is often an indicator of the likelihood of success in other areas of life.

Similarly, Adler regarded all hostile and predatory behavior as also the result of deliberate purpose and intent. According to Adler, people who commit acts of violence, aggression, or other forms of predation and violation are responding to a deep sense of inferiority. Rejection by a social group can cause the subject of rejection to develop a tendency to move in a negative direction that can lead to further isolation, thereby creating a progressive tendency to develop behavior that is unkind, disrespectful, or otherwise undignified.

Adler, Freud, and Jung all subscribed to the philosophy of teleology, which states that all entities have an end function, goal, or purpose. Under this philosophical construct, all human behavior—good, bad, or otherwise—must be regarded as purposive (i.e., serving some practical purpose). As a result, all human behavior, no matter how deviant, can eventually be understood by examining the practical motives of the actor.

Dr. Nuccitelli has been influential in developing the theories of dark psychology. These theories regard the work of Dr. Adler as extremely important. Dark psychology theory agrees that 99.99% of all human behavior is purposive and can be explained through rational means. However, Nuccitelli differs by insisting that that there is .01% of human psychology that is capable of developing harmful and destructive behavior that serves no knowable practical purpose whatsoever. This capacity is what is meant by dark psychology.

There are some important terms that will help readers understand the language of dark psychology, including Dark Continuum, Dark Factor, Dark Singularity. Because this book limits its focus specifically to problems caused by emotional predators and emotional manipulation, we will examine only these three terms in this chapter.

- **Dark Continuum**: Imagine the Dark Continuum as a line used to gauge the nature and severity of behavior based in dark psychology. Mild and purposive acts fall to the left of the continuum, while severe and purposeless acts fall to the right.

   For example, if we use the Dark Continuum to measure the types of conduct that exhibit traits of dark psychology, then psychological and emotional violations would tend to appear on the left side of the continuum, while acts of physical violence would appear on the right side of the continuum.

Of course, an extremely severe emotional or psychological violation committed for purely sadistic purposes may appear further to the right on the continuum than a less severe act of physical violence committed for a rational purpose.

- **Dark Factor**. The Dark Factor is a term used to describe the latent, inherent capacity of all human beings to act with malevolence. This term expresses a theoretical concept to explain the human propensity to develop personality traits that lead to the likelihood that someone will engage in acts of willful violence, destruction, or harm to others.

  There are many influences that may exacerbate or lessen the chance that the latent capacity for abuse will be activated. However, all people possess a Dark Factor in their psychological makeup.

- **Dark Singularity**. This term is also used to describe a theoretical concept. It borrows from the language of physics, which describes a singularity as the absolute center of a black hole. The singularity at the center of a black hole contains energy and gravity that is so dense and powerful that, as objects approach it, they became ensnared in its gravitational pull to the point that they cannot escape. Even light can become trapped in the singularity of a black hole.

Similarly, the Dark Singularity is a concept used to describe the degenerative process that begins by committing acts anywhere on the Dark Continuum. As the actions of a predator increase toward the right end of the Dark Continuum, their psychology becomes increasingly drawn toward further engagement. At some point, they cannot escape the pull of the psychological impulses represented by the right end of the Dark Continuum, and it becomes impossible for them ever to recover a rational state of mind.

To gain a better understanding of dark psychology, Dr. Nuccitelli has compiled the following six tenets that define the nature and function of dark psychology:

1. All people possess the capacity for dark psychology. Dark psychology is not a genetic defect or flaw, but a universal aspect of the human condition.

2. Dark psychology studies the innate human potential for developing predatory behavior that does not serve any

practical purpose. Thus, if 99.99% of human behavior is designed to achieve a practical goal, dark psychology represents that .01% capacity within human psychology to engage in conduct with an end-goal of causing pain, harm, and damage.

3. Dark psychology seeks to fill gaps in the explanation of destructive and harmful human behavior and takes the position that dark psychological behavior traits can manifest themselves anywhere on a continuum of predatory behavior, from mild deviance to extreme violence.

4. The Dark Continuum is not defined exclusively by the end act of deviance or violence, but by the practical, psychological motivations of the person. For example, Jeffrey Dahmer and Ted Bundy were both serial killers. Yet, Dahmer was motivated by the need for companionship and love, however distorted and delusional; while Bundy was motivated by nothing more than a sadistic desire to inflict pain. Thus, Bundy is further along the continuum of dark psychology than Dahmer, even though both were serial killers.

5. Dark psychology assumes that all people have the innate capacity for violence. While animals share this capacity,

they employ violence to serve the needs of the predator-prey relationship in the natural order. Because human beings have evolved beyond that state, yet still retain the innate capacity for violence, this capacity is distorted in human psychology and may be used to act in violence without a practical purpose.

6. By gaining an understanding of dark psychology, human society will be more capable of recognizing, diagnosing, and treating those who exhibit these tendencies and helping them understand that such tendencies need to be channeled in a more productive direction. The more human society masters this aspect of its own psychology, the more it will enable itself to evolve beyond this era of psychological distortion.

Following are four profiles of criminal personality types that have been identified by law enforcement officials and clinical psychologists as exhibiting behavior that exists on the far-right end of the dark continuum:

- **Arsonists**: Arsonists are obsessed with setting fires and commonly have experienced a history of sexual and/or physical abuse. Their dark psychological personality traits are evident in their tendency to live apart from social groups. This isolation tends to further accelerate their decline into self-obsession, which enables them to more easily support their fascination with setting fires. They generally experience a sense of pleasure and happiness when they see their target structures burn.

- **Necrophiliacs**: These are people who exhibit a sexual attraction to corpses. Because necrophiliacs have a difficult time establishing emotional or social bonds with others, their psychological and emotional development is disrupted, and as they move along the Dark Continuum, their attraction to the inanimateness of corpses intensifies.

- **Serial killers**: The FBI defines a serial killer as anyone who commits "a series of three or more killings, not less than one of which was committed within the United States, having common characteristics such as to suggest the reasonable possibility that the crimes were committed by the same actor or actors" (Nuccitelli, 2006).

Clinical psychologists have found that serial killers are motivated by the psychological gratification that can only be achieved through brutality and killing gives them a feeling of released tension and increased power.

- **iPredators.** This term is officially defined as a "person, group, or nation who, directly or indirectly, engages in exploitation, victimization, coercion, stalking, theft, or disparagement of others using Information and Communications Technology [ICT]" (Nuccitelli, 2006). This group of predators represents a new development in the field of dark psychology because ICT has been in use for only a relatively short amount of time.

## Practical and Historical Overview

The foundations of the study of dark psychology are not modern. The models of classical comedy and tragedy during the height of the Greek Empire illustrate an understanding of this uniquely human capacity even during ancient times. The comedies and tragedies of ancient Greek theater were used as a means for society to experience catharsis—a collective exercise in which social bonding occurred by the creation and release of social tensions as a means of resolving societal conflicts.

But what is at the heart of this classical method of employing art as a means of regulating society is society's need to be regulated because of the unique capacity of human beings to act in ways that are destructive and harmful without any apparent practical purpose or necessity. This capacity is what clinical psychologists refer to as dark psychology.

Consider that species other than humans, such as lions, wolves, bears, or birds of prey, may track, target, hunt, and kill smaller, less powerful animals, such as deer, cattle, sheep, rabbits, and rodents. Yet, the reason for this predatory behavior is necessity, not cruelty or malevolence. In addition, when predatory animals hunt, they are likely to target the most vulnerable and the weakest, not out of any sense of meanness or malice, but because engaging with a weaker opponent involves less risk and less effort. Thus, the violence and destruction of natural predators serves practical needs—to feed themselves and their young in an effort to propagate their species.

Especially in the modern world, human beings have the advantage of education, positions of professional employment, the ability to grow and cultivate food, advanced language and communication systems, and a complex and interconnected system of world government, law, finance, and banking. As a result, there is no practical reason for any human being to engage in any act of predation or violence to secure the goals of food, shelter, and propagation. In fact, because the system of laws punishes violence, such actions are actually detrimental to achieving these goals.

These habits and systems of living are unique to the human species, so it is reasonable to assume that they may require responses and abilities among the human members of society that are also unique. For example, lions and wolves are incapable of becoming doctors, plumbers, mechanics, or politicians, nor will they ever have any interest in doing so. These occupations are unique to the human species.

It is tempting to argue that human beings have developed their unique capacity for dark psychology as a means of propagating their survival in this unique environment. Take for instance a business man who cheats on his taxes to gain an advantage in the business world, a lawyer who alters evidence to win a case, or a politician who lies to his constituents to win an election may be compared to the abilities of wild bears who hunt and kill deer or other game. Yet, animals in the wild never engage in predatory conduct that is marked by cruelty, maliciousness, or greed. Doing so would lead to their extinction.

We may understand that a business owner or banking professional would use every tool at his or her disposal to gain a competitive advantage. We may even understand the tendency among some professionals to work around laws rather than follow them when they see an economic advantage in doing so—when no real harm results, there is a practical goal that justifies the apparent abuse.

But often, criminal activity in human society does not have any practical justification. Within the unique sphere of human experience, dark psychology itself is a unique phenomenon. Defined broadly, it is the capacity for destructive and harmful behavior that serves no practical purpose whatsoever.

While all human beings have the capacity for dark psychology, many people do not act on these dark urges, choosing instead to channel that energy toward more productive and useful activities. Some people, however, do act on these dark urges to inflict gratuitous pain and harm on others.

Among those who are governed by dark psychology rather than by rational psychology, there is a continuum of deviant behavior ranging from mild forms of manipulation and dishonesty, usually motivated by some type of personal or financial gain; to acts of physical violence; and at the most extreme end of the spectrum, the movement toward the "Dark Singularity," in which a person's psychology becomes so compromised by and addicted to deviant, aberrant, criminal, and malevolent misconduct that it becomes impossible for them ever to return to a rational mental state.

Historical tales of serial killers like Jack the Ripper remind us that this human failure is not new. Unfortunately, modern society appears to have embraced, at least to some limited degree, a complete rejection of all morality and social norms. The anonymity and access to power and information made possible by the invention of the internet has given these elements resources to establish for themselves a viable, permanent presence in human society. Understanding the nature and function of dark psychology has become an indispensable tool for anyone working to achieve success.

Before considering any further what "dark psychology" means, it may be more helpful to consider what "normal" means. Many historians and literary theorists have made the case that the evolution of human civilization has been accompanied by a steady erosion of social, moral, and cultural norms.

The word "more" (with the "e" pronounced as a long a, i.e., *MOR-ay*) is used to describe the social rules society enforces to encourage acceptable behavior. Many college graduates may remember taking a course from a sociology professor who required as a homework assignment that they deliberately identify and violate a more, then write a paper about the consequences. At one time, it was not uncommon for visitors to a college campus to enter an elevator and find themselves joined by an apparently well-adjusted and successful college student who, for no apparent reason, faced the back of the elevator rather than the doors, thereby forcing uncomfortable and prolonged eye contact. This example of social deviance is very mild and can be viewed as even less threatening when we consider that it occurred in the context of a supervised experiment in the controlled and benign environment of a postsecondary educational institute.

Literature and humanities professors may help students examine this phenomenon in greater, and often more graphic and unforgettable, detail. For example, a pre-internet era literature course at a state university in California examined the transformation of cultural norms from 17th century France up through late 20th century America. In this course, the French novel, *La Princesse de Clèves,* was used to set a ground floor of social norms.

This novel portrays the life of a young woman living in the court of Henry II. Her mother had raised her with the greatest discipline to rise to the height of French society. As she enters adulthood, she is escorted to court to secure a prospect for marriage among the young noblemen. She eventually marries a young prince.

Already at this point in the novel, by today's standards, the main character of the novel would be considered successful beyond the reach of most people. However, her life does not proceed according to the ease and happiness we might expect. Instead, royal intrigue, gossip, and power struggles complicate matters.

Although no actual wrongdoing ever really takes place, the young princess's hopes and ambitions are ultimately destroyed by the mere suspicion of infidelity. She is ultimately motivated by her sense of duty and obligation to enter a convent, where she dies in obscurity.

The course then uses literary works from intervening eras to trace the decline in the standards of human civilization from the virtuous heights depicted in *La Princesse de Clèves* through the dawn of the Industrial Revolution and ultimately to modern society at the end of 20th century America. The endpoint is illustrated by the violence, decadence, chaos, and alienation depicted in the late 20th century American novel, *Looking for Mr. Goodbar*.

In this novel, a young schoolteacher, who, like the princess in the earlier novel, is an accomplished woman occupying an enviable position, is also seeking a prospect. However, her environment—the singles bars of New York City—is far removed from the royal court of 17th century France. Like the princess in the earlier novel, she too suffers a tragic fate at a young age when she is murdered by a young man she has met on one of her social outings.

Thus, defining social norms has become increasingly challenging, and many people have made the case that those norms are eroding as humanity progresses through its evolutionary cycles. We may refer to this tendency to develop destructive, negative, or harmful behavior as "dark psychology." All of the works depicting this trend discussed above existed prior to the invention of digital technology and the internet.

The emergence of iPredators as a class of offenders identified by clinical psychologists underscores the importance of understanding this area of psychology. New technology has expanded the power and speed through which dark psychology has found a way to manifest itself among many segments of human society; ICT has also magnified the degree to which such lifestyles have made themselves potentially viable, long-term means of living.

The following chart illustrates the differences in the psychological makeup between well-adjusted people with healthy psychology and those who exhibit predominantly dark psychological traits:

|  | Light Triad | Dark Triad |
|---|---|---|
| Honesty-Humility (HH)[a,b] | 0.48** | −0.73** |
| HH Sincerity | 0.32** | −0.45** |
| HH Fairness | 0.39** | −0.53** |
| HH Greed_Avoidance | 0.22** | −0.46** |
| HH Modesty | 0.49** | −0.71** |
| Big Five Inventory (BFI)[a,c,d] |  |  |
| BFI Open Mindedness | 0.29** | −0.04 |
| BFI Aesthetic Sensitivity | 0.28** | −0.13** |
| BFI Intellectual Curiosity | 0.21** | −0.03 |
| BFI Creative Imagination | 0.23** | 0.09* |
| BFI Conscientiousness | 0.32** | −0.19** |
| BFI Organization | 0.17** | −0.12** |
| BFI Productiveness | 0.31** | −0.09** |
| BFI Responsibility | 0.37** | −0.29** |
| BFI Extraversion | 0.24** | 0.24** |
| BFI Social Engagement | 0.21** | 0.18** |
| BFI Assertiveness | 0.02 | 0.40** |
| BFI Energy Level | 0.39** | 0.00 |
| BFI Agreeableness | 0.79** | −0.52** |
| BFI Compassion | 0.66** | −0.44** |
| BFI Respectfulness | 0.59** | −0.50** |
| BFI Acceptance | 0.72** | −0.38** |
| BFI Negative Emotionality | −0.30** | 0.04 |
| BFI Anxiety | −0.23** | −0.03 |
| BFI Depression | −0.32** | 0.03 |
| BFI Emotional Volatility | −0.25** | 0.09** |
| Big Five Aspects Scale (BFAS)[b] |  |  |
| BFAS Intellect Openness | 0.36** | −0.05 |
| BFAS Intellect | 0.27** | −0.02 |
| BFAS Openness | 0.34** | −0.06 |
| BFAS Conscientiousness | 0.12** | −0.10* |
| BFAS Industriousness | 0.20** | −0.08* |
| BFAS Orderliness | 0.01 | −0.09* |
| BFAS Extraversion | 0.26** | 0.18** |
| BFAS Enthusiasm | 0.42** | −0.08* |
| BFAS Assertiveness | 0.04 | 0.38** |
| BFAS Agreeableness | 0.68** | −0.58** |
| BFAS Compassion | 0.64** | −0.38** |
| BFAS Politeness | 0.57** | −0.68** |
| BFAS Neuroticism | −0.27** | 0.13** |
| BFAS Withdrawal | −0.23** | 0.05 |
| BFAS Volatility | −0.28** | 0.20** |

[a]Measure included in Study 1 (n = 387); [b]Measure included in Study 2 (n = 670); [c]Measure included in Study 3 (n = 267); [d]Measure included in Study 4 (n = 194). **$p < 0.01$, *$p < 0.05$.

Page **29**

(Comparison of light triad to dark triad, n.d.)

So, dark psychology, in its most general sense, is that part of human psychology that drives people to act in ways that are harmful or deviant. As we have seen, this deviant behavior may range from deliberate but harmless violations of social norms in an educational environment, to mean-spirited rumors spread to defeat opponents, to violent predatory crimes that end lives and lead to severe and long-lasting trauma.

Because a pattern of the evolutionary progress of dark psychology has been identified, clinical psychologists have finally formulated a theory of this type of deviant and dangerous human behavior. In addition, because digital technology and the internet have ushered in an era in which the potential for engaging in deviant behavior has been so dramatically heightened, this body of work will become increasingly important to the survival of human culture and civilization.

# Chapter 2:

# Understanding Dark Triad Personalities

Dark psychology is not a single, universally applicable medical diagnosis that can be applied across all cases of deviant personalities. There are, in fact, a wide variety of ways that dark psychology may manifest itself in someone's psychological and behavioral makeup. There is no absolute division of one deviant personality type from another, and many deviant personalities with prominent features of dark psychology may display elements of more than one manifestation of dark psychology.

This chapter will explore three types of dark psychology personalities. It is important to remember that although the internet has spawned a huge growth in problems resulting from dark psychology, these traits have been part of human culture since ancient times. In fact, one of the dark psychology profiles we will explore in this chapter, Machiavellianism, takes its name from a medieval politician. Another, narcissism, takes its name from an ancient mythological character. Together, the three dark psychology profiles discussed in this chapter—psychopathy, Machiavellianism, and narcissism—make up what is known as "the Dark Triad."

# Psychopathy

Psychopathy is defined as a mental disorder with several identifying characteristics that include antisocial behavior, amorality, an inability to develop empathy or to establish meaningful personal relationships, extreme egocentricity, and recidivism, with repeated violations resulting from an apparent inability to learn from the consequences of earlier transgressions. Antisocial behavior, in turn, is defined as behavior based upon a goal of violating formal and/or informal rules of social conduct through criminal activity or through acts of personal, private protest, or opposition, all of which is directed against other individuals or society in general.

Egocentricity is behavior is when the offending person sees himself or herself as the central focus of the world, or at least of all dominant social and political activity. Empathy is the ability to view and understand events, thoughts, emotions, and beliefs from the perspective of others, and is considered one of the most important psychological components for establishing successful, ongoing relationships.

Amorality is entirely different from immorality. An immoral act is an act which violates established moral codes. A person who is immoral can be confronted with his or her actions with the expectation that he or she will recognize that his or her actions are offensive form a moral, if not a legal, standpoint. Amorality, on the other hand, represents a psychology that does not recognize that any moral codes exist, or if they do, that they have no value in determining whether or not to act in one way or another.

Thus, someone displaying psychopathy may commit horrendous acts that cause tremendous psychological and physical trauma and not ever understand that what he or she has done is wrong. Worse still, those who display signs of psychopathy usually worsen over time because they are unable to make the connection between the problems in their lives and in the lives of those in the world around them and their own harmful and destructive actions.

# Machiavellianism

Strictly defined, Machiavellianism is the political philosophy of Niccolò Machiavelli, who lived from 1469 until 1527 in Italy. In contemporary society, Machiavellianism is a term used to describe the popular understanding of people who are perceived as displaying very high political or professional ambitions. In psychology, however, the Machiavellianism scale is used to measure the degree to which people with deviant personalities display manipulative behavior.

Machiavelli wrote *The Prince*, a political treatise in which he stated that sincerity, honesty, and other virtues were certainly admirable qualities, but that in politics, the capacity to engage in deceit, treachery, and other forms of criminal behavior were acceptable if there were no other means of achieving political aims to protect one's interests.

Popular misconceptions reduce this entire philosophy to the view that "the end justifies the means." To be fair, Machiavelli himself insisted that the more important part of this equation was ensuring that the end itself must first be justified. Furthermore, it is better to achieve such ends using means devoid of treachery whenever possible because there is less risk to the interests of the actor.

Thus, seeking the most effective means of achieving a political end may not necessarily lead to the most treacherous. In addition, not all political ends that have been justified as worth pursuing must be pursued. In many cases, the mere threat that a certain course of action may be pursued may be enough to achieve that end. In some cases, the treachery may be as mild as making a credible threat to take action that is not really even intended.

In contemporary society, many people overlook the fact that Machiavellianism is part of the "Dark Triad" of dark psychology and tacitly approve of the deviant behavior of political and business leaders who are able to amass great power or wealth. However, as a psychological disorder, Machiavellianism is entirely different from a chosen path to political power.

The person displaying Machiavellian personality traits does not consider whether his or her actions are the most effective means to achieving his or her goals, whether there are alternatives that do not involve deceit or treachery, or even whether the ultimate result of his or her actions is worth achieving. The Machiavellian personality is not evidence of a strategic or calculating mind attempting to achieve a worthwhile objective in a contentious environment. Instead, it is always on, whether the situation calls for a cold, calculating, and manipulative approach or not.

For example, we have all called in sick to work when we really just wanted a day off. But for most of us, such conduct is not how we behave normally, and after such acts of dishonesty, many of us feel guilty. Those who display a high degree of Machiavellianism would not just lie when they want a day off; they see lying and dishonesty as the only way to conduct themselves in all situations, regardless of whether doing so results in any benefit.

What's more, because of the degree of social acceptance and tacit approval granted to Machiavellian personalities who successfully attain political power, their presence in society does not receive the kind of negative attention accorded to the other two members of the Dark Triad—psychopathy and narcissism.

# Narcissism

The term "narcissism" originates from an ancient Greek myth about Narcissus, a young man who saw his reflection in a pool of water and fell in love with the image of himself. In clinical psychology, narcissism as an illness was introduced by Sigmund Freud and has continually been included in official diagnostic manuals as a description of a specific type of psychiatric personality disorder.

In psychology, narcissism is defined as a condition characterized by an exaggerated sense of importance, an excessive need for attention, a lack of empathy, and, as a result, dysfunctional relationships. Commonly, narcissists may outwardly display an extremely high level of confidence, but this façade usually hides a very fragile ego and a high degree of sensitivity to criticism. There is often a large gulf between a narcissist's highly favorable view of himself or herself, the resulting expectation that others should extend to him or her favors and special treatment, and the disappointment when the results are quite negative or otherwise different. These problems can affect all areas of the narcissist's life, including personal relationships, professional relationships, and financial matters.

As part of the Dark Triad, those who exhibit traits resulting from Narcissistic Personality Disorder (NPD) may engage in relationships characterized by a lack of empathy. For example, a narcissist may demand constant comments, attention, and admiration from his or her partner, but will often appear unable or unwilling to reciprocate by displaying concern or responding to the concerns, thoughts, and feelings of his or her partner.

Narcissists also display a sense of entitlement and expect excessive reward and recognition, but usually without ever having accomplished or achieved anything that would justify such feelings. There is also a tendency toward excessive criticism of those around him or her, combined with heightened sensitivity when even the slightest amount of criticism is directed at him or her.

Thus, while narcissism in popular culture is often used as a pejorative term and an insult aimed at people like actors, models, and other celebrities who display high degrees of self-love and satisfaction, NPD is actually a psychological term that is quite distinct from merely having high self-esteem. The key to understanding this aspect of dark psychology is that the narcissist's image of himself or herself is often completely and entirely idealized, grandiose, and inflated and cannot be justified with any factual, meaningful accomplishments or capacities that may make such claims believable. As a result of this discord between expectation and reality, the demanding, manipulative, inconsiderate, self-centered, and arrogant behavior of the narcissist can cause problems not only for himself or herself, but for all of the people in his or her life.

## The Dark Triad in Practice

The professional workplace has acknowledged the presence of people exhibiting Dark Triad characteristics. The following diagram illustrates that they are tolerated for their efficiency and their ability to get things done but contrasts that ability with the negative effects it has on their ability to form personal relationships:

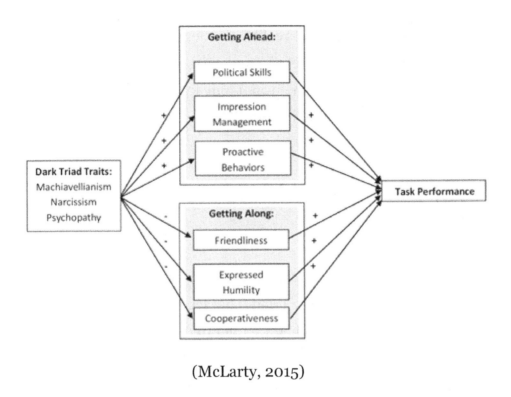

(McLarty, 2015)

The remainder of this book discusses a wide variety of people and situations in which you may find one, two, all three, or some combination of these Dark Triad personalities working in concert around you.

The clinical descriptions are easy enough to categorize, and in isolation, it can be fairly straightforward to separate one type of dark psychology from another. The real world is a lot messier. Many of us have grown accustomed to so-called "toxic relationships," whether they are relationships with our partners, our co-workers, our family members, our bosses, or our political and community leaders. In addition, manifestations of dark psychology arc oftcn far more mundane than the dramatic examples we see in major television and film productions about the romantic lives of serial killers and other criminals. The more we accept these relationships as normal, the more difficult it will be to identify them as problematic.

Remember that psychological, emotional, and social predators do not think of themselves as sick. Their lack of morality and empathy, and their adaption form a very early age to live according to rules and methods you may find horribly wrong, can make their presence intimidating. However, you should also remember that even when their amorality and lack of empathy may allow them to enjoy an unjust advantage in relationships, their mental capacities are the result of underdevelopment, not a higher evolutionary state.

# Chapter 3:

# What is Emotional

# Manipulation?

Now that we have covered the basic foundations of dark psychology, including the concept of seriously dangerous psychopathy and the irreversible movement toward the Dark Singularity, you may feel a sense of relief that these societal problems have been identified, and that a system for addressing them has been established. In addition, you may also breathe a sigh of relief knowing that the most serious offenders are somewhat rare, and that your chances of encountering them on a daily basis are fairly low.

If you agree that knowledge of the traits of dark psychology is a good first step toward protecting yourself from these dangers—that's great! Knowledge is power, more so in the information age than ever.

However, the truth of dark psychology is that lower levels of these deviant personality traits are extremely common. Worse yet, they are often legitimized by the very institutions and people we depend upon to address such violations. Especially in the contemporary environment, in which technology has fostered and encouraged the development of alienation and anti-social lifestyles to the unprecedented degree that they now provide a potentially viable and sustainable means of financial and social support, understanding how dark psychology manifests itself can make the difference between success and failure. As the following diagram illustrates, your ability to establish a high level of emotional intelligence has a direct effect on your job performance:

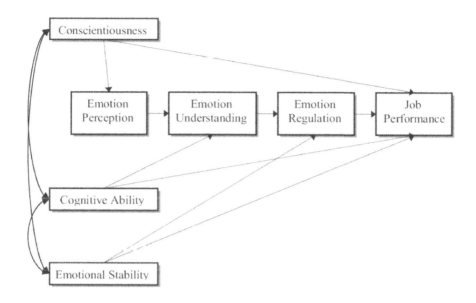

(Effect of emotional intelligence on job performance, n.d.)

In this chapter, we will explore how people who exhibit deviant personality traits may use dark psychology to manipulate and control others.

## Types of Emotional Manipulation

Discussing manipulative behavior accurately requires that we examine this problem from two perspectives: from the perspective of clinical psychology and from the perspective of every-day relationships. We will begin by discussing different types of emotional manipulation using clinical terminology.

Many clinical psychologists have studied and classified manipulative behavior according to well-established theories of behavior modification and cognitive learning. We will look first at some of the techniques identified by a few of these psychologists before looking at real-world examples and signs that someone is trying to manipulate you.

### Characteristics of a Manipulative Relationship

First, one theory states that emotional manipulation is essentially a one-sided activity in which all of the effort to create, execute, and sustain a manipulative relationship is made by the manipulator. Such relationships generally have three defining characteristics:

1. **Concealment**: The true motivations of the manipulator—aggression and control—are concealed by behavior that appears friendly and helpful.

   It is more difficult to conceal problems with aggression and control in our personal, intimate relationships, our friendships, and our relationships among family members. As a result, these types of relationships are more likely to develop in the workplace or in your community among business owners and their staff or other professionals.

For example, you may encounter a co-worker who, on the surface, is always friendly toward you at work. This person may always be willing to find a place for you at the table during lunch break or may always appear at your cubicle with a smile and offer lots of encouragement and advice. This type of conduct in itself may be a good sign. However, if this relationship ultimately leads to a friendship outside of the office, an emotional manipulator may misinterpret your intent.

In the less-regulated world outside of the workplace, emotional predators may exploit the trust they have established by making unreasonable demands on your time, asking for favors, and putting pressure on you to agree by suggesting there could be repercussions at work. A truly gifted manipulator will know how to make this threatening behavior look and feel friendly and perfectly reasonable until you have been too badly compromised to take any action to reverse course.

2. **Profiling**: The manipulator will have studied the vulnerabilities of the victim, so that he or she will be able to exploit them more effectively.

This type of predatory conduct has become much worse in the current environment of surveillance and social networking sites. Later in this chapter, we will examine some of the character traits that make people more attractive targets for emotional manipulation.

Often in the work environment, this type of personality can manifest itself without your awareness. Especially if you work for a large company, anyone who has access to personnel records or other sources of information may feel they have the luxury to profile you so that when they do finally approach, they will appear quite calm and confident.

If someone with whom you have had little or no direct contact seems to know a lot about you, you should be cautious. Often, being overly enthusiastic, paying you a lot of compliments, and telling you that you have earned a great reputation is a technique used to hide the true intentions of the manipulator.

3. **Amorality**: The manipulator will possess high degrees of amorality and a lack of remorse, both of which enable behavior that is ruthless, cunning, and treacherous.

Often, we expect that a simple, polite request to cease harmful, rude, or disruptive behavior should be sufficient to end predatory or violative misconduct. Although we may be right, Dark Triad personalities who lack empathy find it easy to engage in amoral behavior. Even worse, far from feeling any remorse as a result of committing abuses, they often feel a great sense of joy, victory, and accomplishment. As the saying goes, such reactions add insult to injury.

Further, in the competitive business environment, this type of dishonest and illegal behavior may be rewarded. Meanwhile, the efforts of diligent, honest employees may go unrewarded, and their complaints of abuse may result in punishments levied against them rather than the perpetrators.

## Categories of Emotionally Manipulative Behavior

Understanding the basic dynamics of manipulative and abusive relationships is important. Each of these general types of relationships may be characterized by specific types of behavior. Psychologists have identified many specific techniques of behavior modification commonly employed by emotional manipulators. Some of these techniques include:

- **Positive reinforcement:** This technique was identified by the behavioral psychologist B.F. Skinner, whose theory of operant conditioning resulted from his experiments with small animals placed in cages. In his experiment to prove the theory of positive reinforcement, he used cages equipped with two levers—one lever did nothing, while the other produced a food pellet whenever the small animal pushed it. Soon, the animals learned through positive reinforcement which lever to push to get their reward.

  Emotional manipulators employ positive reinforcement in their strategies by using techniques such as praise, false and superficial demonstrations of emotions such as charm and sympathy, excessive rewards including gifts, money, approval, and attention, and other outward demonstrations of emotion meant to make the victim feel good.

- **Negative reinforcement:** The other part of Skinner's experiment proved the effectiveness of negative reinforcement. For this part of his experiment, small animals were again placed in cages, which were again equipped with two levers. This time, the cages were charged with a mild voltage of electricity that caused slight discomfort to the animals that were placed in them. Once inside the cages, the animals would press one of the two levers. One of the levers did not produce any results, while the other stopped the electrical current, relieving the discomfort. Soon, the animals learned to press the lever that lessened their pain.

Emotional manipulators employ negative reinforcement in their strategies by using techniques such as removing someone from a difficult situation or relieving them of the responsibility to complete a previously agreed job or task in exchange for some type of favor.

- **Intermittent reinforcement:** Intermittent reinforcement can be either positive or negative and is used to create doubt, fear, or uncertainty. An emotional manipulator may "train" his or her victim by imposing inconsistent reward and punishment mechanisms to lessen the victim's sense of confidence, control, and autonomy.

For example, in a romantic relationship, the predator may condition the victim to wear certain clothing, listen to certain music, eat certain types of food, and work at a certain type of job. As the victim in this relationship gains confidence, the predator may begin to discourage their victim, who will be caught off guard. As the victim scrambles to respond, the manipulator may again change tactics.

- **Punishment:** Punishment is a very basic form of emotional manipulation that may involve an entire range of psychologically and emotionally negative and damaging behavior, such as threats, yelling, nagging, complaining, intimidation, insults, guilt, and other forms of emotional blackmail. Skilled predators may find a way to incorporate this abusive and controlling behavior into the relationship over time, so that the victim will develop a tolerance for abuse.

- **Traumatic one-trial learning:** This technique is related to the use of punishments, but rather than a feature of a long-term relationship, these techniques involve discrete episodes in which the manipulator uses verbal abuse, demonstrations of anger, and other forms of dominance and intimidation to discourage the victim from certain types of behavior.

## *Specific Types of Emotional Manipulation*

Within these major categories of emotional manipulation techniques, psychologists have also identified a wide range of more subtle variations that we all likely encounter on a daily basis. These techniques include:

- **Lying:** Dark Triad personalities, particularly psychopaths, are highly skilled at lying and cheating, so often we may not detect their intent until it is too late. Beware of those who have demonstrated a pattern of dishonesty.

- **Lying by omission:** Lying by omission is a little more subtle. The predator may not say anything that is untrue but may withhold information that is necessary in an effort to cause you to fail.

- **Denial:** Often the damage from emotional manipulation is inflicted after the fact. When you confront someone with evidence of their dishonesty and abuse, their refusal to admit wrongdoing can cause even greater psychological harm.

- **Rationalization:** The increase in popular news media has led to the growth of public relations and marketing firms who produce "spin" to deflect criticism in both political and corporate environments. Rationalization is a form of spin, in which a manipulator explains away his or her abuse.

- **Minimization:** Like rationalization, minimization is a form of denial in which the predator understates the seriousness of his or her offense.

- **Selective attention and/or inattention:** Manipulators will pick and choose which parts of an argument or debate should be considered so that only their views are represented.

- **Diversion:** Manipulators often resist giving straight answers to questions, particularly when they are confronted by their victim. Instead, they will divert the conversation to some other topic or change the subject altogether.

- **Evasion:** More serious than diversion, a manipulative person confronted with his or her own guilt will often completely evade responsibility by using long rambling responses filled with so-called "weasel words," like "most people would say," "according to my sources," or other phrases that falsely legitimize their excuses.

- **Covert intimidation:** Many manipulative people will make implied threats to discourage further inquiries or resolution.

- **Guilt tripping:** A true form of emotional manipulation, a manipulator will exploit the integrity and conscientiousness of the victim by accusing them of being too selfish, too irresponsible, or not caring enough.

- **Shaming:** Although shaming can be used to bring about social change when large corporations or governments advance abusive or discriminatory policies, manipulators may attempt to intimidate their victims by using sharp criticism, sarcastic comments, or insults to make them feel bad.

- **Blaming the victim:** This tactic has become increasingly common. When a victim accuses a predator of abuse, the predator will attempt to turn it around by creating a scenario in which the victim alone is responsible for the harm that came to him. The predator may also try to accuse the victim of being the aggressor by complaining about the violation.

- **Playing the victim:** Using the opposite tactic of blaming the victim, the predator will lure a conscientious person into a trap by pretending to have been grievously wounded and cultivating feelings of sympathy. The real plan, however, is to take advantage of the caring nature of the conscientious person by toying with their emotions.

- **Playing the servant:** This tactic is common in environments marked by a strict, well-established chain of command, like the military. Predators become skilled at manipulating this system by creating a persona of suffering and nobility, in which their bad actions are justified as duty, obedience, and honor.

- **Seduction:** This technique does not always have to involve sexual conquest or intimacy. Emotional predators may use flattery and charm to convince people to do their bidding, and they often look for people with low self-esteem.

- **Projection:** This term is used in psychotherapy. Predators who use this technique will look for victims to use as scapegoats. When the manipulator does something wrong and is confronted, he or she will "project" his or guilt onto the victim in an effort to make the victim look like the responsible party.

- **Feigning innocence:** This technique can be used as part of a strategy of denial. Under questioning, the manipulator will "play innocent" by pretending that any violation was unintentional or that they were not the party who committed the violation. A skilled manipulator who lacks morality and empathy can be very successful at planting the seed of doubt.

- **Feigning confusion:** This technique can also be used as part of a strategy of denial. Under questioning, the manipulator will "play dumb" or pretend to be confused about the central point of the conflict or dispute. By creating confusion, the manipulator hopes to damage the confidence of his or victim.

- **Peer pressure:** By using claims, whether true or not, that the victim's friends, associates, or "everyone else" is doing something, the manipulator will put pressure on his victim to change his or her behavior or attitude.

## Signs That You're Being Manipulated

All of us are potentially susceptible to emotional manipulation by people who exhibit characteristic signs of dark psychology. Victimization can occur in our everyday relationships with co-workers, bosses and supervisors, family members, and significant others. Emotional manipulation can also occur in professional relationships with people we may regard as normally trustworthy—such as sales representatives, government officials, and other representatives of institutions such as medical facilities, banks, businesses, schools, and law firms.

Emotional predators share one common trait: They look for people whom they know are conscientious, dependable, loyal, honest, and reliable. People with these character traits are the easiest to manipulate because all of the tricks in the manipulator's toolbox are designed specifically to take advantage of these emotional and psychological characteristics. More importantly, emotional predators lack empathy or morality. They do not regard their abuses as shocking or unacceptable; instead, they regard the overabundance of conscientious people as "job security" and a golden opportunity.

Emotional predators can be found in all walks of life. Over the course of their lives, they have learned how to adapt, blend in, and even achieve high levels of professional and financial success in the "straight world." Remember that having a valid and legitimate expectation that people will be honest in their dealings with you means that you are a conscientious person. Although you occupy the superior position, emotional predators are highly skilled at exploiting this expectation and avoiding detection and/or punishment.

As we have seen, emotionally manipulative people use a wide variety of techniques and methods to gain power in relationships. What's more, the people you are closest to and most familiar with—people whom you should be able to trust the most—are in the best position to use emotional manipulation to exploit and take advantage of your trust. In fact, establishing trust and familiarity is one of the most important aspects of a successful effort to exploit someone's emotional vulnerability, then manipulate them either for personal gain or simply out of pure malice.

Of course, simply because this type of abuse has become common does not mean that you should automatically and necessarily regard all of your friends and trusted associates as predators and manipulators. Nor should you give into the temptation to regard being conscientious, law-abiding, and honest as a problem. However, victims of emotional manipulation are often unaware that they are being exploited and abused, so it is important to learn how to recognize the signs of manipulation.

By finding ways of resolving disputes and conflicts that are healthier, or by devising an exit strategy to protect yourself from any further damage, you will achieve a greater degree of happiness and success and can avoid many of the problems that plague people who are unaware of what is happening to them or who have been intimidated into not reacting.

Whether in your work life or your personal life, you may have been exploited or violated by an emotional predator. The prevalence of this deviant behavior and the degree to which it has become regarded as acceptable is unsettling, to say the least. The following list departs from the more theoretical and clinical descriptions of predatory behavior above to provide more vivid examples of the type of conduct that may indicate the presence of emotional manipulation.

### Specific Examples of Emotional Manipulation

- **Insisting on meeting at certain locations:** Manipulators may try to get the upper hand by insisting on a so-called "home court advantage," thereby forcing you to function in a less familiar and less comfortable environment that diminishes your personal negotiating power.

  ***Examples:***

  ○ If you have a dispute with a professional acquaintance or colleague, they may insist on always meeting in their office or at a café or restaurant that is more difficult for you to travel to.

- If you are in a personal relationship, you partner may always insist that you meet him or her at their favorite spot and meet with their friends. They may show little interest in reciprocating when you invite them to participate in social activity you find rewarding.

- **Premature intimacy or closeness:** The manipulator will immediately shower you with affection and reveal all sorts of intimate secrets.

*Examples:*

- In a personal relationship, the manipulator may introduce themselves using phrases like, "No one has ever made me feel like this before. I know we were made for each other."

- This type of intimacy and closeness can happen in the professional environment, too. A colleague you don't know very well may make comments like, "You know, I have been watching you work, and I can see how skilled and talented you are. No one else really gives you the credit you deserve."

- **Managing conversations by always requiring you to speak first:** In professional relationships, this is commonly used as a sales and negotiation technique to mine you for your information to make a more lucrative sale.

  *Examples:*

  - A salesperson may say something like, "Rather than bore you with details about our products or services, why don't you tell me about yourself and how you think we can help you?"

  - In personal relationships, this technique can be used to gain a power advantage. Skilled manipulators will conceal their true motives by saying things like, "I may have been wrong, but first I'd like to hear your side of the story."

- **Distorting or twisting facts:** Whether in personal or professional relationships, manipulators will use conversational techniques to distort facts in an effort to make you doubt yourself and back down.

  *Example:*

  - A manipulator may use a phrase like, "I understand how you feel. I'd be angry, too. But the truth is, I never made that comment. I don't think your memory of that conversation is accurate. I know what you really meant to say was that..."

- **Intellectual bullying:** An emotional manipulator may use an unnecessarily large volume of statistics, jargon, or other types of factual evidence to impose a sense of expertise.

  *Example:*

  - Someone who is implementing the tactic of intellectual bullying may say something like, "This is not an easy decision to make. In addition to all the legal and financial considerations, you also have to consider how this will affect people at work and the rest of the family. I know technology is not your strong point, but I have already done all the heavy lifting in that regard. Now, we only have a limited amount of time, and I know how important this is for you. I wish we could just take our time and think about it. Fortunately, I have already evaluated all the major concerns, and I can make it really easy for you to make a decision."

- **Bureaucratic bullying:** This technique is similar to intellectual bullying. Unfortunately, this technique may indicate that someone is abusing their position of authority by insisting on placing as many obstacles, red tape, or other impediments in the way of what should be a straightforward resolution.

*Example:*

- o Such a person may make a statement such as, "I understand your concerns, but I would encourage you not to pursue this any further. You have a legitimate complaint, but the expenses and time required will likely cost more than you will get in return. Also, if you make any missteps, you may have to spend the next several years filling out paperwork and going to court hearings."

- **Passive aggression**

   There are many examples of passive aggressive behavior in conversation in both personal and professional relationships to force you to back down to the predatory efforts of a manipulator.

   *Examples:*

   - o A manipulator may try to make you feel bad for voicing your concerns by saying something along the lines of, "I understand that you are voicing an important objection, but have ever stopped to consider what will happen to the rest of the team if you eventually get your way?"

- Manipulators may also try to discourage you by making light of your problems. For instance, "I know how bad you feel right now, but before you do anything, make sure you keep it in perspective. You know, this time last year I was facing a crisis ten times worse, and all I did was sit it out."

- **Insults and put-downs:** Manipulators are good at following up rude or mean-spirited comments with sarcasm or some other attempt at humor to make it seem like they were joking.

  *Example:*

  - "I know you really worked hard on that presentation. It's too bad you wasted your time, though. But, hey, no worries. I'm sure it will be great preparation when you interview for your next position."

- **Refusing to take responsibility:** There are a variety of ways a skilled manipulator can accomplish this goal by using evasion, denial, or feigning ignorance or confusion.

*Examples:*

- "You didn't tell me I had to finish the project by today."

- "I know that's not what you wanted, but everyone else agreed that it should be fine this way."

- "What do you mean by accountability? I don't remember discussing any of that with you."

- "Can you explain the problem with this project again? It's really too hard for most people to understand."

- **Competitive responses:** Manipulators may introduce outside, unrelated issues to convince you that your concerns are less important.

*Example:*

- "I do understand you've been placed in a difficult situation, but you should think about me. Right now, you have already passed all the sales goals I wanted to achieve for this year. It's bad enough that you're making me look bad. Now you're forcing me to ignore my own workload just so I can help you out."

- **Excessive criticism:** Hypercritical people often have problems with low self-esteem. They will use this technique to make them feel better about themselves. Often these efforts can be very blatant, obvious, and hurtful.

  *Examples:*

    - "You shouldn't wear that. It makes you look fat and ugly."
    - "You shouldn't talk so much in meetings. You usually just end sounding stupid."

- **Projecting blame:** Manipulators can place you in a position in which you are forced to take responsibility for their actions.

  *Example:*

    - "I know that meeting didn't go the way you had hoped. I tried to tell you not to pick me to lead the meeting. Next time, you should listen to me."

- **Using guilt and ultimatums:** Manipulators do not have to resort to physical violence. Often, delivering an ultimatum while making you feel bad can force you to act in ways you otherwise wouldn't.

*Example:*

- ○ "Remember what happened last year when I asked you to decide where to go for the Christmas holiday? The entire holiday was ruined because you took too long to decide, and then you made everyone stay home instead of taking the trip back home. This year is going to be different. If you don't decide by the end of the day, we're never going to invite you to another Christmas party again."

- **Indirect communication:** This has become an increasingly common technique used by manipulators and bullies and often involves the use of gossip and rumors.

*Example:*

- ○ "You can forget about the funding for that project we had planned. I know you told me to wait until the meeting tomorrow, but I already talked to the boss and told him it was a bad idea."

- **The silent treatment:** In the connected world of digital communication, many manipulative people will simply ignore text messages, email messages, and voicemails as a way of letting you know they do not approve of something you have done.

- **Gaslighting:** The manipulator will make blanket statements to draw your credibility and judgement into question. Manipulators are highly adept at lying, then imposing the falsehood on you until you accept it and back down.

*Examples:*

Suppose you are at work, and you have documented a pattern of workplace violations that are costing you time and money. The manipulator may try to gaslight you by first requesting to see the evidence with a sincere expression of concern.

- o "I see. You definitely have a very convincing case. Let me see if I can find out what's going on so we can get to the bottom of it."

Subsequently, using a combination of denial, indirect communication, and feigned ignorance or confusion, the manipulator may return to you in a couple of weeks with a different response.

- o "I know I agreed with you at first. But I was talking to the other guys. I think you might have a couple of the dates wrong. Also, I know it seems like a big deal, but most of the other guys were saying they do this kind of thing all the time, and it's never a problem. Wait, what was the law or rule or whatever you were talking about again? It seemed really important when you were talking about it, but no one else seemed to know anything about it. I don't know... Maybe you're just overreacting."

- **Using negative surprises:** Many people in both personal and professional relationships will use "negative surprises" to maintain power in a relationship and manipulate and control people.

### *Example:*

In the workplace, you may have been encouraged by members of management to follow a specified path that will lead to a promotion and a raise. After you have put in overtime and gone above and beyond to meet all the demands, the boss makes an announcement at the meeting where you expect to be promoted:

- o "I know James has been working very hard these past few months, and we all appreciate his inspirational efforts to increase our sales numbers. I am also glad you are all here to hear who will be promoted to the position of District Manager. We just got word this morning that I will be personally assuming the new role, while also maintaining my current position."

- **Playing the martyr:** Manipulators use this technique to establish control.

*Examples:*

A manipulator's initial reaction when you ask them to help with a special project might be:

  ○ "Sure! Great! Let me know how I can help!"

However, once the assignment or project is underway, their comments will be entirely different.

  ○ "I know I said I was eager to help, but this is really too much. This workload is such a burden. I wish I had never agreed."

You may respond by reminding them that you discussed all the details ahead of time and criticizing their resistance, but their response will likely place the blame on you.

o "Of course, I agree. Really, it's not a problem. You're just being overly sensitive and paranoid. You shouldn't worry so much."

The goal here is to make you look like the bad guy, call your credibility into question, and undermine your authority.

# Factors That Make You Vulnerable to Manipulation

The other side of avoiding the trap of toxic relationships with emotionally manipulative people is to consider whether you have any of the personality traits predators look for in those they are most likely to victimize.

Many of us expect to be treated with respect and kindness and according to the basic laws and customs of educated, civilized, responsible adulthood. We take this understanding for granted and expect for it to be a given in all of our relationships. We consider this to be the default understanding in our relationships not only among those we know and trust, but perhaps even more so among strangers, co-workers, and professionals with whom we may come into contact. Unfortunately, emotional predators are well aware of this expectation and often exploit this area of trust specifically when looking for ways to exploit victims.

We have all seen films about the nice-looking stranger who asked for help with a flat tire or the new neighbors who seemed so nice when they first moved in. Slowly, these relationships that seem so benign and normal on the surface quickly spiral into a seemingly inescapable nightmare of violence, victimization, and criminality. Though we are right to regard these types of relationships as the exception rather than the rule, they have unfortunately become more common. As a result, becoming more self-aware is an equally important aspect of avoiding manipulation and exploitation as looking for signs of abuse in those around you.

The following list covers many of the characteristics that emotional manipulators consider weaknesses and will try to exploit. If you believe you may display any of these characteristics, remember that it does not mean you are a weak person or deficient, nor does it mean that you deserve to be exploited or manipulated. However, you should remember that, right or wrong, if you are too open about these types of behaviors, you may be placing yourself directly in the path of an emotional manipulator who is looking for a new victim.

- **Over-eagerness to please other people:** Often a competitive work environment or even the natural environment of your personal relationships rewards achievement. Normally, that's a good thing. But take care to monitor for changes in the environment. People who naturally work to achieve success can be taken advantage of by being placed in a disadvantageous position.

- **Addiction to earning approval and recognition:** This trait is different from the trait of the narcissist, who feels entitled to excessive approval and recognition, even without having done anything to earn it. Yet, demonstrating an addiction to recognition and approval may signal to anyone with high degrees of dark psychology that you are an easy target.

- **Fear of expressing negative emotions:** Often manipulators will identify people who want to avoid repercussions from complaining about or standing up to abuse because they may fear the rejection that results. This trait is also known as emotophobia. Be careful that you are not intimidated into allowing people to violate your rights.

- **A lack of assertiveness or the inability to say no:** This trait is related to emotophobia, but it has more to do with your ability to set personal or professional boundaries and limits, rather than your ability to respond to the behavior of those around you.

- **A low degree of self-reliance or self-sufficiency:** Manipulators will look for people who need help because they represent a wide-open target for long-term victimization. Knowledge is power.

- **Absence of self-direction:** "Locus of control" is a term used to describe the degree to which someone is self-directed or whether they require the direction and control of some external authority or person to make decisions. People who tend toward having more of an external locus of control are more susceptible to emotional manipulation and exploitation.

- **Persistent naïveté:** Being trusting, innocent, and naïve is not in itself a negative character trait. However, the degree to which someone persists in the delusion that they cannot be harmed by predatory behavior, even when it has been made clear to them that they are being exploited and manipulated, can make it difficult to resolve instances of abuse.

- **Over-conscientiousness:** This trait is related to persistent naïveté. When someone knows they are in a manipulative or abusive relationship, an overly conscientious person may continue to give the abuser the benefit of the doubt.

- **Low levels of self-confidence or self-esteem:** People with little confidence are often singled out by manipulators because they will be more susceptible to flattery and deception out of desperation.

- **Over-intellectualization:** This is the mirror image of intellectual and bureaucratic bullying. For example, someone may be an obvious victim of bureaucratic bullying and continue to receive official communication promising resolution if the victim will continue to cooperate. If the victim over-intellectualizes the abuse by accepting the official-looking nature of the communication as proof of the predator's good intentions, then the exploitation will likely continue.

- **A dependent or submissive personality:** People who are naturally less assertive and who respond well to care and love should not feel ashamed or that they are doing something wrong. However, a predator who identifies submissive personality types may successfully exploit such people without their being fully aware of the abuse. Often, the need for companionship and love may make otherwise shrewd and intelligent people uncharacteristically gullible and vulnerable.

- **Emotional and intellectual immaturity:** Immaturity, like naïveté, can result in a greater likelihood that people will believe exaggerated claims or promises.

- **Impressionability:** This trait is related to immaturity. Impressionable people may be susceptible to predatory abuse simply as a result of a charming or persuasive presentation or introduction.

- **Carelessness:** When honest people finally learn to adjust their responses to account for manipulators and predators, they may still run the risk of carelessness. Their newfound awareness of the treachery of the surrounding world may fill them with a sense of righteousness or entitlement—since they are not the predators or criminals, they should not be held responsible for changing their behavior. Although they may be right, failing to maintain vigilance after a real and present danger has been established can open the door to more abuse.

- **Narcissism:** Ironically, narcissists themselves can become victims of their own psychological deviance. Because of their obsessive need for flattery, they may be targeted by those who seek to disarm them using false flattery to gain their trust and respect.

- **Impulsiveness:** This is another trait that honest, naïve, and trusting people must learn to curtail. Although they may be right that they should not have to fear the constant presence of predatory manipulation, failing to conceal impulsiveness can leave them vulnerable to cons and other traps.

- **Altruism:** This trait is also respectable and admirable, but people who are overly altruistic and selfless become easy targets for predators who lack empathy.

- **Greed or materialism:** Negative personality traits can also make people susceptible to victimization. The contemporary environment celebrates materialism, greed, and consumerism. Because society has been engineered to make these attitudes acceptable and desirable, vast segments of the population have been set up as victims of financial criminals and other dishonest businesses run by people displaying the personality characteristics listed in the Dark Triad.

- **The elderly:** Elderly people are frequent targets of emotional manipulation. This applies especially to honest people who have maintained vigilance for a long period of time. Their success in having avoided victimization may give their confidence a boost, which may tempt them to let their guard down. In addition, the physical problems associated with aging may make them more fatigued and less able to maintain high levels of awareness.

# Chapter 4:

# Dark Persuasion Methods

The previous chapters have described some of the worst-case scenarios of how dark psychology and the people who exhibit its most negative and anti-social characteristics may enter our lives and cause considerable harm. Such examples may range from the extreme horror of serial killers, stalkers, and other deadly, predatory criminals to comparatively less harmful, more common, but still dangerous personality types who may exert emotional manipulation to get what they want from you.

All of these examples are always present in the world around us, some more common and frequent, others less so. All of them can cause trauma and damage to our lives ranging from simple, mild annoyance, to financial damage or job losses, to serious physical injury and loss of life. These examples all share something in common—they are generally examples of behavior that represent, at the very least, violations of established codes of moral and social conduct, and at the very worst, violations of laws, from petty misdemeanor violations to felonious civil and criminal violations.

But not all manifestations of dark psychology occur in the shadows, in dark alleys, in bad relationships that no one likes to talk about, or otherwise out of plain sight. In fact, much of the human capacity for dark psychology has been legitimized by non-profit organizations, educational institutes, medical facilities, private corporations, and even government agencies to enable a wide range of programs based on psychological manipulation.

That being said, not all efforts to change people's behavior can or should be regarded as negative. For example, at the most harmless level, so-called social influence may be as benign and even desirable as the way parents teach their children from a young age or how children learn from their teachers at school. Similarly, you may have friends or family members who have offered you friendly advice at some time in your life when you faced an important decision or were about to do something that in hindsight could have been a big mistake. In these cases, social influence in the form of someone telling you that you should or shouldn't do something is an indispensable ingredient to success.

Of course, there are more large-scale social influence campaigns. We are surrounded by advertising campaigns from multi-billion-dollar corporations, each of which wants us to buy this product or that product. And a large part of the efforts of many government agencies are directed at shaping public opinion, including changing behavior. In some cases, like convincing people not to drink and drive, to wear their seat belts, or to help fight forest fires, require huge educational efforts and long-term public relations campaigns with repeated messaging to convince people by tapping into both their conscious and subconscious awareness that changing their behavior is in their best interest.

Chapter 3 discusses how people use language to distort facts and use communication as a means of emotional manipulation to force people to do what they want. The examples outlined in Chapter 3 illustrated how a lack of awareness of the power of communication can make us susceptible to emotional predators. Certainly, such toxic relationships should be avoided.

Probably everyone at one time or another has been in a relationship with someone who used these techniques. However, the truth is that not all practitioners of emotional manipulation are malevolent, shadowy figures lurking in dark offices of big-city high-rise office buildings. Many people make a living as life coaches and professional development trainers. Many people employed as sales representatives by major corporations may be required to attend personal influence seminars to learn how to polish their presentation skills. These individuals may be employed by your employer's human resources department. Many such organizations can be found in the office suites of professional buildings alongside accounting firms, dental offices, and other businesses. The business of influencing people is itself a big business.

This chapter will discuss three major areas in which well-established and officially recognized organizations use the human capacity for dark psychology in various programs of behavior modification. These include neuro-linguistic programming (NLP), hypnosis, and brainwashing.

# Neuro-Linguistic Programming and Non-verbal Communication

During the 1970s, a new social and cultural movement was established, in which the virtues of self-improvement and the development of one's full human potential were cited as a sort of

Holy Grail of higher education. These movements were associated with so-called New Age Spirituality, which challenged traditional beliefs of established Western religious and social conventions.

For example, success in one's personal and professional life have traditionally been regarded as the result of external recognition of one's efforts. Whether God rewards someone's virtuous conduct, or whether society's institutions recognize the value of someone's professional contributions, the key to success in personal and professional life have generally followed from people's ability to conduct themselves according to the established standards and traditions of the larger societies and belief systems in which they live.

New Age Spirituality and the Human Potential Movement attempted to establish an alternate route to success. These new schools of thought used scientific advances in linguistics, political science, technology, sociology, psychology, and medicine to argue that people no longer needed to depend on external recognition for success in any area of their lives. Instead, the general theory was that all people are born with an innate ability to succeed in any area of life, and that the key to unlocking success lies in an individual's ability to harness the power of positive psychology, thereby empowering them to achieve success at anything simply by virtue of perfecting their own unique human psychological and intellectual characteristics.

The school of NLP emerged during this time. The Esalen Center in Northern California was a famous liberal think tank through which the founders of NLP generated hundreds of thousands of dollars in book sales and therapy and training workshops. The NLP foundation has produced several books, which sold hundreds of thousands of copies. Although it eventually became notorious for its pseudo-scientific methods and theories based on little, if any, actual scientific proof or evidence, self-help has become a multi-billion-dollar global industry, and NLP and the many self-improvement businesses and training programs it inspired are still very much a part of the professional and political landscape.

### What Is NLP?

Neuro-linguistic programming is a system of education and training based on an understanding of developmental, behavioral, and cognitive psychology. Education and training in NLP focuses on three aspects of human psychology: the neurological system, which regulates the physical functioning of the human body; language function, which determines how we interact with other people; and "programming," a term used to describe the beliefs, knowledge, and experiences we accumulate over time that together inform our worldview and determine how we behave.

NLP was originally founded in the 1970s by John Grinder and Richard Bandler. The theories behind their work are based in both the scientific study of linguistics, sociology, and political science, as well as New Age mysticism and the self-improvement movement that also began in the 1970s. Specifically, their claim that the "map is not the territory," as a way of describing the disconnection between our subjective perception of the world and reality itself are taken directly from the work of Alfred Korzybski, who founded the school of general semantics in 1933.

In addition, they reference Gregory Bateson's work detailing the conflict between flaws in societal and governmental systems and how they can cause problems in human communication and government. Finally, the work of Noam Chomsky, whose theories of transformational and universal grammar linked the important influence language function has in areas as seemingly unrelated as world government and politics, is one of the primary theories used to support claims that NLP therapy can transform the lives of its followers.

NLP is also influenced by many non-scientific movements, including the mystical writings of Carlos Castenada. Many sociologists have categorized NLP not only as a pseudo-science, but also as a quasi-religion that belongs to the large sphere of New Age and/or Human Potential movements. Some have criticized NLP as a form of folk magic that borrows the language and theories of science and medicine to validate practices that are completely non-scientific.

Carlos Castaneda wrote a series of novels in the 1970s portraying the power of shamanism among the indigenous tribes of North America, and many of the NLP modeling techniques borrow directly from Castaneda's novels, including "double induction" and "stopping the world." NLP behavior modification techniques based in modeling and the use of NLP language coaching use mimetics similar to the rituals of many New Age syncretic religions.

There is a basic philosophical assumption underlying all of the human potential and self-improvement programs that originated during the time NLP was developed. Objectivism is a philosophy based on the understanding that reality is a fundamental, physical fact—the material world that surrounds is objective reality, and we can come to an understanding of this reality through our senses. More importantly, objectivism insists that reality is the same for everyone because it is objective. Though individual perceptions may differ, the objective reality does not.

The philosophies upon which NLP is based take a radically different approach and may be regarded as subjectivism. The basic theory is that each of us is incapable of knowing reality, because we all perceive the world subjectively, filtered by what we have learned from previous experiences and cultural and traditional learning. In addition, the part of the world we live in is governed by laws and customs we have come to know as "true." But these laws and customs differ from one geographical location to the next, and from one demographic group to the next. Thus, for each of us, the world is limited because we can only perceive it from a limited and subjective perspective.

According to the founders of NLP, your thoughts, feelings, and beliefs are not things that actually exist; they are things that you have learned to do. Because we have spent so many years of our lives learning how to do these things from the people around us, our neurological systems, at some point, accept them as reality. We stop questioning whether other facts or perspectives exist, or, using the language of NLP, whether there are other facts and perspectives that would help us to do other things. In the language of NLP, this is known as an internal "map of the world" that we learn through sensory experience.

We learn to communicate using both verbal and non-verbal language. The words we use, the metaphors we are most comfortable with, the analogies that are most common in our speech, our vocabulary, our level of discipline in using correct grammar or pronunciation, the amount of slang we use, whether our language is casual or formal, the ideas we talk about, the accent we are most likely to use when speaking—all of these linguistic abilities follow directly from our map of the world. Although this dual form of communication is very complex and powerful, our ability to communicate is limited by this subjective experience of reality. Together, these two elements, our neurological maps, which in turn form our patterns of linguistic expression, represent our "programming," hence, neuro-linguistic programming.

Below is a diagram illustrating the theory behind NLP:

# NLP Model of Therapeutic Change

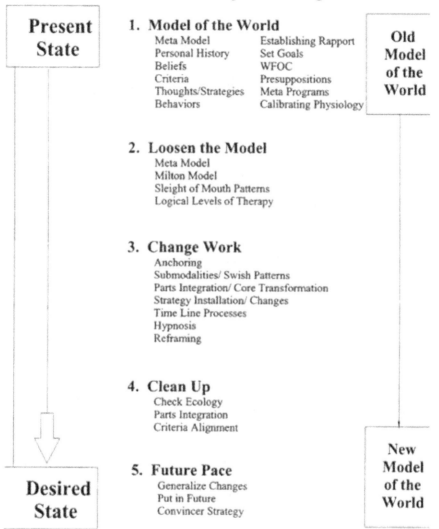

**Present State**

**1. Model of the World**

| Meta Model | Establishing Rapport |
|---|---|
| Personal History | Set Goals |
| Beliefs | WFOC |
| Criteria | Presuppositions |
| Thoughts/Strategies | Meta Programs |
| Behaviors | Calibrating Physiology |

**Old Model of the World**

**2. Loosen the Model**
Meta Model
Milton Model
Sleight of Mouth Patterns
Logical Levels of Therapy

**3. Change Work**
Anchoring
Submodalities/ Swish Patterns
Parts Integration/ Core Transformation
Strategy Installation/ Changes
Time Line Processes
Hypnosis
Reframing

**4. Clean Up**
Check Ecology
Parts Integration
Criteria Alignment

**New Model of the World**

**5. Future Pace**
Generalize Changes
Put in Future
Convincer Strategy

**Desired State**

(NLP model of therapeutic change, n.d.)

## *Verbal and Non-verbal Communication*

When most of us think of language, we think of English or Spanish or Chinese or French or whatever other language we may be fluent in. For most of us, language is simply what we use to communicate ideas—whether basic facts about objects and directions, more complicated information involving technical, legal, or medical terminology, or highly developed figurative language to express abstract concepts and ideas. Language has rules, and we either follow the standardized rules of grammar and usage, speak a colloquial or regional dialog that uses altered language forms, or we adapt language use and invent new forms and uses to suit whatever communication need we may have. But because our perceptions are limited, our linguistic abilities are also limited. As a result, our programming limits our ability to achieve goals in our personal and professional lives.

Another aspect of language is non-verbal communication. Words and sentences themselves only comprise part of the entire process of sending messages and communicating. According to Gregory Bateson, one of the language theorists that influenced the development of NLP, 8% of information we communicate results from the words we use, the other 92% uses non-verbal cues.

If words are the digital component of communication, non-verbal cues are the analog counterpart. These analog aspects of communication include voice tone, tempo, and volume. Other non-verbal cues may include facial expressions, gestures, posture, and eye contact.

Non-verbal communication uses what are called "meta-messages" that provide detailed "editorial" information about the context or motivation for the words of the speaker and help the listener determine how to interpret the message. For example, if someone in a meeting spilled coffee on his computer and it stopped working, he might say, "That's just great!" If he uses a sarcastic tone of voice, he will communicate the opposite message that the words themselves convey. Or if a teacher in a classroom says "I want you to pay attention, now," while pointing at a whiteboard, the message will be entirely different than if the same teacher says, "I want you to pay attention now," while pointing at his ears.

Although only 8% of communication is verbal, the 92% of non-verbal cues usually occur out of the awareness of the speaker. As a result, NLP training sessions spend a lot of time helping people adapt their non-verbal behavior patterns. The theory is that they may not be getting what they want because they are communicating the wrong message, and by communicating a different message, those around them will respond differently as well.

In addition, according to theories of NLP, language serves a far more complex function than merely allowing us to communicate facts or even more elevated and abstract concepts. NLP theory holds that the human capacity for linguistic development is important because our "body states are revealed in our language and non-verbal communication. Language is the tool we use to gain access to the inner workings of the mind," not just a method of communicating with other people. Thus, the promise of NLP is that using "language patterns [can] teach us how to access unconscious information that would remain vague and unknowable otherwise."

### How does NLP work?

The basic premise of NLP is that people who are experiencing difficulties in their lives are really being held back because their internal "maps" tell them they are either incapable or not allowed to engage in whatever type of activity they may have set as a goal for themselves.

In a session of NLP training, an experienced NLP practitioner works with the client by eliciting both verbal and non-verbal language to detect the biases, beliefs, and limitations inherent in that person's map. The NLP practitioner then uses specific techniques to help the client change certain behavior patterns and beliefs so that he or she will no longer feel that certain behavior or associations are off the map are out of their territory.

A typical NLP session is based on "modeling," in which the subject who wishes to use NLP to transform his or her behavior is coached by a certified NLP trainer. NLP has become a widely used and varied program of professional and personal development; there is no single, certified, or regulated method of practicing the behavior modification techniques of NLP. Some of the techniques most commonly used in NLP sessions include:

- **Anchoring**: A sensory experience, or a location on the map, is used as a starting point to trigger emotional states leading to change. For example, if the NLP practitioner finds that a client has difficulty finding motivation at work, but not at home, then finding the sensory experience that triggers motivation at home can be used as the anchor to provide the client with a way to access motivational drive at work.

- **Rapport**: After eliciting various language cues to assess the client's internal subjective map, the NLP practitioner can match physical behavior, non-verbal expression, and language cues to create a bond of empathy.

- **Swish pattern:** Once certain patterns of behavior have been identified, that is, once the NLP practitioner identifies the familiar routes the client takes through his or her map, the goal with the swish pattern is to change the pattern of behavior to create more desirable outcomes.

- **Visual-kinesthetic dissociation (VKD)**: If an NLP client is experiencing negative thoughts and feelings as a result of some past event, this technique is used to isolate the subjective sensory experience and separate it from the memory.

A typical session involves several stages, beginning with the establishment of rapport between the client and trainer. During this stage, the trainer elicits information from the client using specifically designed language and non-verbal communication techniques. Next, the trainer uses "meta-model" questions to gather information about the client's current state of affairs, listening not only to the words the client uses to respond, but also interpreting non-verbal cues according to NLP-based interpretation of their significance.

The client is encouraged to "visual" his or her ideal state of success and the trainer's hope is that by changing his or her mental focus, the client's responses, both verbal and non-verbal, will reveal the secrets that are holding them back. The trainer also begins to use "pacing" by leading the client toward change using specifically designed vocabulary and non-verbal cues in an effort to retrain the client and help them learn to use different verbal and non-verbal communication methods.

NLP also encourages the use of self-reflection. The client is coached to begin envisioning his or her desired future state, and how those changes may affect his or her current personal and professional life. Next, the trainer helps the client change their internal beliefs about the world, i.e., helps them reprogram their worldview. In the final change, the client begins rehearsing their new role in the world to understand how they will be different when all of the changes are finally complete.

According to NLP, these isolated sessions result in behavior modification that will, of itself, inevitably lead the client to successfully implement the changes he or she desires at the conclusion of NLP therapy.

## Is NLP Effective?

Although based in valid, recognized, and established scientific research in sociology, linguistics, and psychology, the theories of NLP have been largely discredited as pseudo-science. The founders of NLP based their theories on sound scientific research, but the scientific community has stated repeatedly that the founders' comments and responses to inquiries have demonstrated that they do not understand the underlying theories they often cite in their work. In addition, they have not produced any of their own original scientific evidence either to support the claims made by NLP theorists, or that their programming sessions actually bring about the changes they promise.

Mainstream psychology has established through clinical research, practice, and published works the reality of the subconscious mind and the importance of understanding its function to help alleviate, treat, or change harmful psychological developments in individuals. Cognitive behavioral therapy (CBT) and traditional psychotherapy must meet with fairly rigorous professional standards and is based on proven methods and theories of clinical psychology, while NLP's record of success is less consistent and based more on anecdotal testimony.

NLP providers generally have a financial interest in promoting the success of NLP, so their testimonials may or may not be true. In addition, results among people who have completed NLP training sessions are mixed. Some studies have shown that patients who participate in NLP have improved psychological symptoms and better quality of life, but the majority of studies indicate there is little evidence that NLP can effectively treat any significant psychological disorders, such as anxiety, insomnia, or substance abuse.

However, while clinical studies have discredited NLP as a legitimate form of treatment for serious psychological illnesses, NLP continues to be part of the large, profitable industry that capitalizes on the demand for self-improvement literature. Tony Robbins, the contemporary self-help, self-improvement, and motivational speaking guru, trained with NLP's founders and continues to employ many of their ideas in his famous seminars.

Regardless of all the negative press reports and scientific criticisms, NLP has spawned a global industry. Companies such as NLP Power, The NLP Center, The Empowerment Partnership, and the founders' own NLP University continue to advertise and promote their services on the internet and provide behavior modification training to a global audience. In addition, many corporations and government agencies send employees to NLP-based seminars in their efforts to train leadership teams and sales staff. Thus, while the scientific foundations of NLP have been exposed and discredited, these organizations continue to attract followers and clients who see a benefit in the behavioral changes that result from associating with organizations that provide training in psychological and behavioral change.

# Hypnosis

### *What is Hypnosis?*

Whereas NLP is a pseudo-science, hypnosis and hypnotherapy have been accepted by the medical establishment as viable methods of behavior modification and therapeutic psychological treatment. Hypnosis is also referred to as hypnotherapy or hypnotic suggestion.

According to the Mayo Clinic, hypnosis is defined as "a trance-like state in which you have heightened focus and concentration...usually done with the help of a therapist using verbal repetition and mental images."

The word hypnosis is derived from the Greek word "hypnos," which means "sleep." There is some debate about who first developed the theory and practice of hypnosis. Many people believe hypnosis was first developed in the 19th century. Some people credit the French researcher Étienne Félix d'Henin de Cuvillers who had spent time trying to understand how people in a deep state of relaxation would respond to suggestions to change their behavior. Others have credited James Braid, a Scottish surgeon who has been given credit for first calling the practice "hypnosis."

Many of the humorous and negative stereotypes of hypnosis can be credited to 18th century German physician Franz Mesmer. Mesmer conducted many experiments and demonstrations in his efforts to prove what he referred to as "animal magnetism." He believed an invisible fluid flowed between living animals, people, and plants, and that by influencing the direction and rate at which this fluid flowed, he could create behavioral changes. His attempts to prove this so-called "animal magnetism" were eventually discredited, and his practices were shown to be dishonest and lacking in any scientific validity. However, his earlier efforts eventually led to further research. In addition, his influence has been long-lived—we still refer to excellent artistic performances or engrossing dialog as "mesmerizing."

Contemporary hypnotherapy consists of two functions: Induction and suggestion. During hypnotic induction, the therapist attempts to place the patient into a deep state of relaxation. Once the patient has achieved a hypnotic state, the therapist makes suggestions designed to help the patient achieve the desired behavior. The following diagram illustrates the degree to which we are influenced by our subconscious mind, the reason so many people turn to hypnotherapy to help them change deep-seated behavior:

# THEORY OF THE MIND

*"How Hypnosis and Suggestibility Works"*

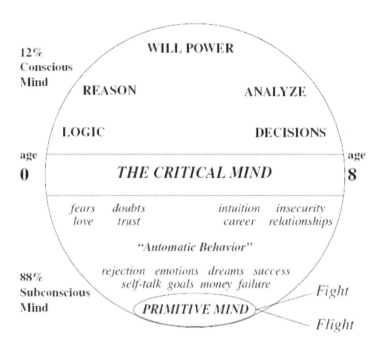

12%
Conscious
Mind

WILL POWER

REASON          ANALYZE

LOGIC          DECISIONS

age
0          *THE CRITICAL MIND*          age
8

*fears   doubts          intuition   insecurity
love   trust          career   relationships*

*"Automatic Behavior"*

*rejection   emotions   dreams   success
self-talk   goals   money   failure*

88%
Subconscious
Mind          *PRIMITIVE MIND*          *Fight*

*Flight*

**Right Brain Suggestibility:** The Emotional and creative side that listens literally but speaks inferred.
**Left Brain Suggestibility:** The logical and detail side listens inferentially but speaks literally.

(Model of hypnosis, n.d.)

## What Are the Uses of Hypnosis?

Patients under hypnosis feel calm and relaxed and are generally more open to suggestions. The main uses of hypnosis are for resolving problems associated with physical illnesses, behavioral problems, and psychological ailments.

- **Physical conditions:** Hypnotherapy can help patients who are having difficulty with any of the following physical illnesses:

### Chronic or acute pain

Many patients who have been diagnosed with rheumatoid arthritis or post-surgical pain have benefited from hypnotherapy by altering the patients' perception of pain. In one experiment, a patient under hypnosis was instructed not to feel any pain in his arm. The patient then placed his arm in a tub of very cold ice water and was able to leave it therefore several minutes without experiencing any pain. Patients in the same experiment who had not been hypnotized had to remove their arms from the water after only a few seconds.

### Pain associated with medical procedures

Patients who are undergoing dental care, childbirth, or other painful medical procedures have benefited from undergoing hypnotherapy prior to treatment.

### Migraine headaches

Because migraine headaches are often triggered by stressful conditions, hypnotherapy can help reduce their frequency and intensity without the side effects of medication.

### Irritable bowel syndrome (IBS)

This condition can cause considerable discomfort. Although not effective as a long-term treatment on its own, hypnotherapy can help patients resolve short-term discomfort associated with IBS.

### Side effects from cancer treatment

Chemotherapy to treat certain forms of cancer can cause considerable discomfort and nausea. Hypnotherapy has been effective in helping some patients alleviate these side effects.

***Skin conditions, including warts, psoriasis, and eczema***

Some skin conditions can be triggered by stress and anxiety. In these cases, helping patients find a way to resolve chronic anxiety can help relieve symptoms.

- **Behavioral changes:** Hypnosis can also be used to effect behavioral changes, such as in treatments for the following conditions:

***Insomnia***

Patients suffering from insomnia may also be suffering from stress-related conditions. Hypnotherapy can help patients learn new habits and techniques to help the patient fall asleep without medication.

***Smoking, overeating, bed-wetting***

Addictions and other behavioral problems can be difficult to resolve using only therapy and medication. Hypnosis can help patients learn to change their behavior in areas where they have been resistant.

- **Emotional and psychological disorders:** Finally, hypnotherapy is sometimes used to treat the mental health problems listed below.

### Stress and anxiety

Stress and anxiety disorders are often treated with medication. However, such treatment may only address symptoms and may result in harmful side effects. Hypnosis can provide an additional source of relief for patients suffering from this condition.

### Phobias

Phobias are a difficult and complex area of psychology. Though there is no single answer for why someone may have developed a certain fear, hypnotherapy can help the patient change his or her perceptions and reactions to triggers.

### Post-traumatic Stress Disorder

Also known as PTSD, this condition is similar to stress and anxiety disorders but usually caused by an acute or sudden traumatic experience. The effects can cause long-term problems and hypnotherapy can help patients find healthier ways of responding.

### Grief and loss

Grief and loss can lead to ongoing challenges for many people. By helping patients refocus their attention, hypnotherapy can aid in a quicker recovery.

### *Depression*

There are many causes of depression. Sometimes patients have been in difficult circumstances, while others may be psychologically predisposed to depression, Often, it is a combination of factors. Regardless, hypnosis can help patients redirect their mental focus and find relief.

### *Dementia*

Patients with dementia may have trouble concentrating and remembering. Hypnosis has been shown to be effective at helping them reconnect with familiar surroundings.

### *Attention Deficit and Hyperactivity Disorder (ADHD)*

The growing concerns about this psychological ailment have resulted from the quickened and disjointed pace of work and life in environments that use digital technology and video. Hypnosis can help patients adjust to a less stressful setting and develop a longer attention span.

## *Myths About Hypnosis*

Dispelling the many stereotypes of hypnosis is the first step in understanding this area of psychotherapy. The sideshow practitioner with a big moustache who dangles or spins a large object with a spiral design in front of the patient until they fall under his spell occurs only in movies.

- **Myth #1—Patients cannot remember what happens during hypnosis.**

  It is not true that patients under hypnosis cannot remember anything when they are pulled back out of the hypnotic state. Patients under hypnosis are generally fully aware of everything during hypnosis and remember everything that occurs during a session.

  In some cases, as when a hypnotherapist suggests to the patient that he or she forgets certain things that occurred immediately before or during a session, the patient may experience posthypnotic amnesia, but this effect may result from a deliberate effort to help the patient recover from a psychological difficulty, and in most cases it is limited and temporary. Amnesia has been reported in some cases, but it is very rare.

- **Myth #2—Hypnosis can help patients remember forgotten events.**

Television crime shows often portray the power of psychics and hypnotherapists to solve crimes by helping traumatized victims recall details from the crime scene that allow lawyers and police officers to crack the case, but the idea that hypnosis can help patients retrieve forgotten details or memories of past events has been largely disproven.

There is some evidence that hypnosis can help improve memory overall. However, studies have shown that in instances in which hypnosis has been used to help patients retrieve lost memories or achieve so-called "past life regression," the results were more likely false memories or fictitious recollections resulting from suggestions during the trance state.

- **Myth #3—Hypnotherapists can put you under a spell and make you do anything.**

It is a myth that anyone can be hypnotized against their will or forced to act in ways that violate their beliefs or morality. In order for hypnosis to be effective, the patient must be a willing and active participant. Similarly, when the patient is fully hypnotized, the hypnotist does not have complete control over the actions of the patient under hypnosis. People who are hypnotized may be less inhibited to act in certain ways, but even in a trance state, patients are not able to act in ways they believe are wrong or that violate their morals or ethics.

- **Myth #4—Hypnosis can give patients superhuman abilities.**

  Popular culture sometimes portrays the limitless possibilities that can open up to patients who undergo hypnosis. Film and television may portray hypnotherapy sessions in which the patient is convinced that when he or she comes out of the trance state, they will be able to run faster than a car, be smarter than anyone else at work, lift automobiles, or resist bullets. Hypnotherapy can help patients improve their performance in a variety of areas—both physical and mental. But it cannot allow anyone to exceed the limits of their own physical or intellectual abilities.

### Facts About Hypnosis

In actual practice, hypnotherapy is much less dramatic and exciting than the portrayals in popular film and television. In fact, many people enter a hypnotic state every day. A hypnotic state is defined as a very relaxed and focused psychological state in which the subject is very calm, focused, susceptible to suggestion, and less likely to be influenced by hesitations or inhibitions.

For example, every time you sit down at home or in a movie theater to watch a film, you enter a hypnotic state. As the movie begins, your mind shifts its attention from concerns about work, family, relationships, bills, and other daily concerns to the story that is about to unfold. Especially if the lights are dimmed and outside interference from sounds and activity is muffled or blocked, your mind gradually relaxes and begins to shift its focus more and more to the film, until at some point you are entirely engrossed by the images, sounds, and events on the screen. Often during these episodes, we enter such a deep state of hypnosis that we react to scenes of violence, comedy, or shock as if they were actually happening.

In professional environments, many contemporary work gurus have developed the idea of "flow." When you are at work and so focused on what you are doing that it ceases to require any strain or effort, you have entered a state of "flow." When you are in this state, you are capable of producing high quality work that may normally seem excessively difficult. What's more, you may be able to sustain this high level of productivity for hours on end and even derive an intense sense of pleasure and happiness. This, too, is a state of hypnosis.

Hypnosis is usually used in combination with psychotherapy. During psychotherapy, patients may have explored many of the painful or difficult thoughts or feelings they have been experiencing. Under hypnosis, they may be more willing to explore these areas in more depth, which can lead to a better resolution. There are two main types of hypnosis:

- **Suggestion therapy:** This type of hypnosis uses suggestions to help patients change their behavior, as with smoking or overeating, or to change their perceptions, as in cases when patients are experiencing pain and discomfort.

- **Analysis therapy:** This type of hypnosis is used to put patients in a deep state of relaxation, so they will feel more willing to discuss some of the thoughts and feelings that may be hidden in their subconscious mind. This type of hypnosis can be used to help treat psychological and mood disorders, especially when it is used just prior to a session of psychotherapy.

# Hypnotherapy

## *What Happens During Hypnotherapy?*

During a typical session of hypnotherapy, the therapist will begin reviewing the patient's goals for treatment. Once you and the therapist are clear about the reasons for seeking hypnotherapy, he or she will begin talking in a calm, soothing, and gentle voice, usually describing images and scenes to help the patient relax and feel safe. This initial step is designed to create what is called a "receptive state" in the mind of the patient. Once the therapist sees you have attained this state of relaxation and receptivity, he or she will begin suggesting ways you might achieve your goals. These suggestions may include constructing visual images in your mind in which you see yourself successfully attaining the behavior or condition you have identified as your goal.

For example, the session may begin with the therapist asking you to close your eyes, relax, and let go of any tension. Depending on the personal information you have shared with your therapist, they may then begin to suggest locations or events that you associate with feelings of safety, relaxation, and calm—maybe the beach or the ocean, a room in your home, or some type of music or activity.

Once the patient has achieved a trance state, which is described as a state between sleep and wakefulness, the hypnotherapist can make suggestions. If the therapist suggests that you are eating a cheeseburger, you may experience the meal and taste of a cheeseburger, if the therapist suggests that your nose is heavily congested from a cold, you may alter your voice when you talk. Alternatively, the therapist may ask deep and probing questions about a sensitive area of your life that you normally are uncomfortable discussing. In a hypnotic state, you may find it much easier to open up.

Throughout the session of hypnotherapy, the patient feels a complete lifting of inhibitions. He or she will be very suggestible and willing to act in ways that normally be embarrassing or uncomfortable. Yet, at no time does the patient lose consciousness or forget that he or she is engaged in a session with a hypnotherapist. The effectiveness of hypnotherapy lies in its ability to induce the patient to enter a state in which their inhibitions have been lowered so that the psychological defenses they have built up no longer prevent them from saying or doing things that can help them resolve their problem. With enough practice and training, many patients are eventually able to practice self-hypnosis as part of a program of ongoing self-care.

### Is Hypnotherapy Effective?

As discussed above, hypnosis is used in a fairly limited number of situations to help people cope with pain, stress, depression, grief, or anxiety; certain physical ailments like irritable bowel syndrome; overcome the effects of chemotherapy associated with cancer treatment; or to effect behavioral changes such as quitting smoking and losing weight.

Generally, although hypnotherapy has been recognized as having valid and proven clinical results, it is still viewed as a supplementary or secondary line of treatment following a full program of psychotherapy or cognitive behavioral therapy.

In addition, some people are more likely to benefit from hypnotherapy than others. People who exhibit higher levels of activity in the prefrontal cortex, the anterior cingulate cortex, and the parietal regions of the brain are more likely to be suggestible under hypnosis. These areas of the brain regulate functions such as memory, perception, emotions, and task learning. Overall, researchers have developed the following statistical analysis of the effectiveness of hypnosis in the general population:

- Approximately 15% of people report high degrees of responsiveness to hypnosis.

- Approximately 10% of adults are resistant to hypnosis or impossible to hypnotize.

- People who exhibit the capacity to indulge in fantasies generally experience more benefit from hypnosis.

- Children are usually easier to hypnotize than adults.

## *Drawbacks of Hypnotherapy*

In certain cases, hypnosis may actually cause harm.

For example, patients with symptoms of psychopathy or who experience hallucinations or delusions may be hard to control or may experience a worsening of their condition under hypnosis. Some psychiatric disorders may require the use of medication, and in these cases, hypnosis may be an ineffective treatment. Hypnosis is also not recommended for patients who are currently abusing substances or under the influence of drugs or alcohol.

Patients who wish to use hypnosis as a method of pain control should be examined by a physician first to ensure they are not experiencing any serious problems that may require surgical or medical intervention.

Finally, due to hypnotherapy's ability to cause the patient to create false or fictitious memories or to experience strong emotions, using hypnosis to treat patients with serious psychological disorders, such as those outlined in the Dark Triad or other dissociative disorders, is generally regarded as potentially harmful and dangerous.

# Brainwashing

### What is Brainwashing?

If hypnosis is the benevolent uncle of social influence techniques, brainwashing is the red-headed stepchild. Technically, "brainwashing" is not a term that has been officially accepted either by the legal, scientific, or medical communities.

Currently, those seeking to legitimize studies in this area of human behavior control have developed the more accurate term, "coercive persuasion." Other terms include thought control, re-education, thought reform, menticide, and mind control. Regardless, brainwashing is a term used to describe efforts to forcibly and radically change someone's beliefs, values, views, and attitudes using a combination of physical violence and psychological manipulation.

Notice that in hypnosis, no patient who is unwilling to enter a suggestive state can be hypnotized, and no hypnotherapist can force any unwilling patient to become hypnotized. Brainwashing represents the antithesis.

Theoretically, brainwashing techniques are employed precisely in situations when the subject is most unwilling to change his or her behavior. In these cases, brainwashing techniques are used specifically to force the subject to change against their will and without their full knowledge or consent.

According to the Merriam Webster Online Dictionary, "brainwashing" has two distinct definitions:

1. A forcible indoctrination to induce someone to give up basic political, social, or religious beliefs and attitudes and to accept contrasting regimented ideas.

2. Persuasion by propaganda or salesmanship.

### The History of Brainwashing

Historically, the term "brainwashing" was coined to describe the forcible conversion of an individual from one set of ideological, political, or religious beliefs to another. Because the brainwashing process requires the use of force and is understood as a process in which the subject is an unwilling participant, it requires the use of extensive and excessive behavior modification tools and techniques. These techniques may include:

- Efforts to control the subject's physical environment. This control may be exerted by forcing the subject to inhabit a prison cell or some other location that is physically isolated. The brainwasher controls physical access to the location, so the subject is either not free to leave or is subjected to constant monitoring.

- Efforts to control the subject's social environment. For example, the subject may be isolated from associates, friends, and family members, combined with limitations and controls on the type of news and information they may access.

- A daily regimen designed to impose unquestioning obedience to authority and absolute humility. Such regimens may require daily sessions of "education" or indoctrination in which all responses are closely monitored, without any tolerance for dissent or deviation.

- A system of social rewards and punishments to pressure subjects into conforming to the new ideology.

- A system of physical and psychological punishments to deter non-conformity. Such punishments may range on the mild end of the spectrum from social rejection, shunning, criticism, and ostracism; to more serious actions like deprivation of food, sleep, or social contact; to extreme actions like physical beatings, bondage, stress positions, and torture.

- All brainwashing systems require continual reinforcement to achieve their objectives.

In this sense, the goal of brainwashing is to forcibly convince the subject that their way of thinking is incorrect, to completely break down and eradicate their former personality and worldview, and then to replace their psychological makeup by rehabilitating them with rewards, punishments, and re-education to encourage a change in behavior.

The term "brainwashing" first came into use during the American Cold War in reference to the emergence of communism and the eventual communist takeover of China. In 1950, the *Miami Herald* published a story entitled "Brain-washing Tactics Force Chinese Into Ranks of Communist Party." The article stated that Mao Zedong, the Chinese communist leader, had used ancient methods of torture to force the Chinese people to become mindless drones of the communist political and military machine.

The article also warned that everyone was now susceptible to these techniques that could turn anyone, anywhere into a human robot serving alien, hostile, or foreign interests. Worse still, there would be no external evidence to the casual observer that someone had been brainwashed. This story preceded earlier American political movements to suppress the spread of communism by prohibiting people that had been identified as having political or social views described as liberal, socialist, or communist from working in schools, libraries, journalism, or entertainment.

Subsequently, during the Korean War against the communist state of North Korea, which was part of the larger Cold War, a high-ranking American military officer was shot down, captured, and, along with many other prisoners of war, held in prison camps run by agents of communist governments.

A year after this high-profile event, many of these American POWs had signed false confessions in which they stated they had committed a series of war crimes against North Korean civilians. Through the media, the American public expressed shock. This reaction worsened when 5,000 of the 7,200 known American POWs petitioned the U.S. government to end the war.

The height of terror came when 21 of the POWs refused to repatriate after their release, choosing instead to remain in communist territory. At this point, the threat of brainwashing became very real and very palpable, and these fears have contributed to American domestic and foreign policy disputes ever since.

Films like *Invasion of the Body Snatchers* and *The Manchurian Candidate* are classics of American theater and have popularized notions that the threat of brainwashing is everywhere and often undetectable. The American political and intellectual establishment struggled to come to an understanding of how this apparent radical shift in the worldviews of so many people had occurred, and finally legitimized the theory by including brainwashing as a dissociative disorder in the Third Edition of the Diagnostic and Statistical Manual of Mental Disorders (DSM-III).

However, scientists who studied the behavior of the POWs in prison camps during the Korean War concluded that the behavioral change had a simpler explanation—the soldiers who had signed false confessions had been tortured. In reaction to these events, the military became convinced that its soldiers were simply weak and needed to be trained to resist efforts at brainwashing. As a result, they developed a program known as the Survival, Evasion, Resistance, Escape program, or SERE, which was designed to prepare soldiers for resistance against future efforts at brainwashing and indoctrination.

Another respect of brainwashing that is often overlooked is the long legacy of human experimentation that occurred during the 20th century. In America, prisoners, people from poor and marginalized populations, people with intellectual impairments or thought or mood disorders, newborn children, and many others were often unknowingly and unwillingly subjected to medical and scientific experiments in an effort to develop vaccines or test psychological or behavioral theories.

The former Soviet Union also conducted many controversial scientific experiments on its vast population of political prisoners. Nazi Germany also routinely used Jewish prisoners in concentration camps to conduct human experiments to test a wide variety of theories. Some of these experiments were a direct result of the emergence of the fear of communist brainwashing and were developed as official intelligence programs administered by the Central Intelligence Agency (CIA).

For example, MKUltra was the code name for a CIA-backed research program that existed from 1953 until 1973. Under the guise of fighting brainwashing, the CIA involved test subjects without their knowledge by using them to test mind-altering substances like LSD, hypnosis, sensory deprivation, psychological and sexual abuse, and even torture. The CIA used facilities at hospitals, universities, prisons, and other private and public institutions. The theoretical justification was to develop drugs and brainwashing techniques for use in clandestine operations, but the program was eventually shut down after a congressional investigation.

Regardless, the idea that brainwashing should be part of a comprehensive package of international diplomacy has been part of American military, political, and intelligence policies in virtually every conflict since the end of the Cold War, and many of those policies are still in use today.

Despite the shuttering of MKUltra by Congress in the 1970s, many of the techniques developed during that time were employed in post-9/11 interrogations of terrorism suspects at Abu Ghraib Prison in Iraq and in Guantanamo Bay in Cuba. The War on Terrorism began with a brutal interrogation of a suspected Al-Qaeda terrorist using the playbook of Cold War counterespionage and brainwashing techniques that included physical torture, sleep deprivation, and other forms of behavior control, which led to a series of confessions by the subject, all of which turned out to be false.

## Brainwashing Today

The misadventures of military and intelligence agency officials convinced of the power of brainwashing and torture to uncover valuable information that will protect national security interests has been in the news almost constantly for many years. However, brainwashing is also defined as "persuasion by propaganda or salesmanship" and its more subversive presence has resulted from the increasingly cultish nature of contemporary American society.

Less dramatic examples of brainwashing occur on a much more frequent and regular basis in everyday American society. American life has become increasingly cultish or, as some people prefer to say, tribal. Because of massive corruption and ongoing news stories of political crimes, scandals, and failures in virtually every American institution, many people have become disillusioned.

Because we all have a need for social acceptance, and cannot help but respond to the demands and needs of modern society, many people who believe they are simply building successful careers and establishing a network of friends and associates do not realize they have been recruited by a cult until they are so isolated from their friends and family that legal or even military intervention is required to extract them. In addition, even the family members and friends of those who have joined cults and died fighting for the ideals of their leaders may argue in all these cases whether any brainwashing was actually involved. Often, people act on their own initiative to join cults or new religious movements of their own free will.

For example, during the 1970s, Patricia Hearst, an American heiress and daughter of the prominent and powerful media magnate William Randolph Hearst, was put on trial and sentenced to prison for her part in having joined a domestic terrorist organization and taking part in violent criminal attacks. During her trial, she claimed she had been brainwashed. However, the court was disinclined to regard claims of brainwashing as a valid defense for several reasons.

Primarily, the foundations of brainwashing were tenuous and shadowy, so proving a claim of brainwashing according to the standards of established legal precedent is extremely difficult. In addition, the courts were not eager to establish such a precedent because they feared it would open a floodgate of defendants claiming, "not guilty by reason of brainwashing."

Although the court rejected her defense, most people regarded her case sympathetically. She had been kidnapped and held at gunpoint by an armed gang, so her case stood out as the most obvious case in which a brainwashing defense might be regarded as valid. She received a reduced sentence and was eventually pardoned for her part in the crime.

Another example of brainwashing by cultish indoctrination is the Unification Church, a religious organization headed by the Reverend Sun Yung Moon, or "The Moonies." Often portrayed sarcastically and comically in American films, many Americans have told stores of joining the Moonies as a reaction to disillusionment and lack of purpose in their lives.

In one such case, an American college student said that despite having been raised Jewish, he was quickly convinced that the Moonies were going to succeed in their efforts to save the world and became what he described as an "off-the-charts, fly-a-plane-into-the-World-Trade-Center-if-Father-ordered-you-to Moonie," (Father is the title cult members use for the Reverend Sung Yun Moon). According to this cult member, he "was sure they wouldn't be able to make [him] betray Father. [He] wanted to prove to [his] parents that [he] was not brainwashed or mind-controlled." Eventually, however, he left the cult and became a mental health counselor specializing in treating and counseling other former cult members.

Yet another example of a contemporary religious cult is The People's Temple that was run by the Reverend Jim Jones. He had led his followers to Jonestown, Guyana in 1978. Jones and his followers were highly idealistic and vehemently opposed many of the corruptions and abuses of the political establishment. They ran into tremendous opposition from family members and members of Congress.

As two members of Congress flew to South America to intervene in what they saw as a potentially dangerous and worsening situation, almost 1,000 of the cult members in attendance chose to commit suicide by voluntarily drinking poison-laced punch, hence the term "drinking the Kool-Aid" to express the idea of incomprehensible indoctrination.

The fate of Branch Davidians under the leadership of David Koresh in Texas was similarly apocalyptic, with Branch Davidians choosing to die as martyrs for their belief in the sanctity of David Koresh's preaching rather than surrender to American military forces.

Yet even in these examples, many of the surviving participants, their family members, and experts in the field argue about whether or not these cases are examples of brainwashing, since those who join these cults often do so as an act of free will. In addition, many cultish associations emerge in ways that are less visible.

The social psychologist Alexandra Stein joined a political organization called "the O." At the time, she did not know that it was a cult, but the organization wielded considerable control over her life throughout the 1980s. In addition to keeping her sleep-deprived by requiring her to hold multiple jobs, she was also isolated from her friends. In retrospect, she blamed vulnerabilities resulting from her own sense of loss and confusion and only realized later that the cult leaders were exploiting her.

In addition, the rise of social media, with all of its highly personalized, targeted advertising has allowed big business to capitalize on the idea of brainwashing as "persuasion by propaganda or salesmanship" to unprecedented degrees. Advertising is nothing new, but mainstream marketing and advertising has moved from newspapers, television, and radio into the personal lives of virtually everyone.

The U.S. military's huge budgets supporting research and development in digital global satellite communication, combined with successful marketing campaigns that have made Apple, Microsoft, and Google more powerful than many sovereign governments, and the use of Big Data Analytics to tailor advertising to extremely high levels of scientifically accurate psychological profiling have transformed the advertising and marketing business. Even President Barack

Obama once commented that U.S. spies no longer want to kill people, they want to sell products.

Unfortunately, many of the erosions and breakdowns in traditional society, such as gender roles, challenges to authority, and a general sense of lawlessness and absence of accountability, combined with digital technology's capability of encouraging increasingly isolated and alienating individualized lifestyles, mean that all of us are increasingly susceptible to the malevolent abuses of brainwashing and cult recruitment.

## Challenges of Brainwashing in the Future

Following from the previous section, brainwashing is a difficult area in which to gain any firm understanding. Its origins as a reaction to the unprecedented rise of communism in the 1950s makes it a fairly new development in human psychology.

Most psychologists agree that it is possible to successfully brainwash an individual or a group of individuals. However, they also agree that popular portrayals of brainwashing are inaccurate, both in terms of the likelihood of success and in terms of the severity of the influence. Specifically, the extreme measures and the extreme goals of brainwashing rarely occur unless they are deliberately created. Furthermore, as patients who willingly undergo hypnosis to recall repressed memories have been found more likely to simply invent fictitious memories, so subjects of brainwashing are not likely to undergo any real conversion, except conversions that result from forcible, violent threats and torture.

In addition, government programs like MKUltra have been shown to produce unreliable results. Such political and military failures and catastrophes should result in the cessation of such abuses, but often they do not. However, arguments supporting the use of indoctrination and brainwashing will lose ground as long as their use continues to perpetuate these problems.

Regardless, the increasing presence of cults in American society is certainly a cause for concern. Unregulated groups beyond the reach of oversight agencies often operate according to alternative worldviews not based on legally or psychologically sound philosophies. In addition, the rise of digital technology and social media have given them more communication tools that will likely only increase their power and ability to recruit new members.

However uncomfortable it may be, we must also acknowledge that even the people we know and love the most may have beliefs we never really understand or agree with that may lead them to join groups that support alternative lifestyles. Brainwashing cannot always explain these actions; maintaining our freedom and independence requires that we must all be willing to tolerate the risk of dissent.

As long as society continues to develop according to cultish patterns, encourages greater social alienation and isolation, and fails to ensure political and legal accountability, unregulated social influence will continue to pose potentially grave risks.

# Chapter 5:

# How to Protect Yourself Against Emotional Predators

So far, this book has explored a wide range of practical and theoretical research about how dark psychological personality traits may manifest themselves in people, as well as why we should all be concerned about how these personality traits may pose a potential risk to each of us. This chapter will explore some practical methods of detecting the presence of emotional predators, how to prevent them from causing the kinds of conflicts and disruptions they are likely to cause, and how to recover from encounters with people who exhibit these personality traits.

However, before we discuss the specific, practical details of successfully dealing with emotional predators, it is important to place all the information in the preceding chapters in an appropriate context. Thus, the first section of this chapter will discuss the nature of emotional psychology and why it is important, how contemporary social and professional environments pose unique challenges, and where emotional predators fit in.

# Emotional Psychology as a Necessary Ingredient for Success

According to Mark Leary, PhD., in an article published in the Dialogues in Clinical Neuroscience and the U.S. National Library of Medicine and the National Institutes of Health, "[i]nterpersonal rejections constitute some of the most distressing and consequential events in people's lives." This assertion may seem counterintuitive. After all, every day each of us will likely experience a very high number of social contacts ranging from long, complex interactions with people with whom we share a very close or intimate bond to casual encounters with people who are familiar to us to short, quick exchanges with strangers, clients, customers, or other professionals who together comprise the social universe we inhabit.

Generally, when we think about "distressing, consequential events," we think about catastrophic illnesses, significant disruptions to our financial or professional well-being, or the death or serious illness or injury of ourselves or loved ones. So, it may seem an overstatement to include interpersonal rejection in the category of events that we might consider "the most distressing and consequential."

However, Dr. Leary goes on to offer a convincing argument for the basis of this theory, an argument that may also help you develop both an awareness of how important maintaining healthy emotional psychology can be and understanding the importance of social interaction to your own personal and professional success.

Charles Darwin's *The Expression of the Emotions in Man and Animals* was an important contribution to theories examining emotional psychology and predation, and gave rise to theories of so-called "social Darwinism," from which popular culture derives its belief in the "survival of the fittest" ethos and the predominance of ruthlessness and cut-throat policies as the foundation of business success. However, the more important theme of these theories of human development is that "emotions

[are] ... evolved adaptations that provide an advantage to survival and reproduction... In particular, emotions signal the presence of events that have potentially major implications for ... well-being—specifically, important threats and opportunities in [a given] ... environment—thereby causing the individual to focus on concerns that require immediate attention."

Furthermore, though we scarcely ever think about it consciously, emotions like embarrassment, hurt, and loneliness can often signal threats or challenges that emerge as the result of our complex interrelationships. Both acceptance and rejection are social responses to our own individual behavior.

When we experience the acceptance and approval of those around us, we are overcome with positive emotions such as confidence, and we generally are satisfied that we have somehow made the right choice or satisfied some standard that will allow us to move ahead in our lives. Conversely, when we are rejected, whether by receiving negative feedback in the form of a professional proposal that is rejected, a social invitation that is declined, or being entirely expelled by a social group, we may be overwhelmed with feelings of guilt and shame. Especially when we believe we have been rejected for reasons that are not defensible or justified, we may also experience a great deal of anger.

In a normal, healthy social environment these signs of social acceptance or rejection occur without a lot of pre-meditation or conscious thought—they are simply a natural reaction among groups and individuals within groups to behavior that either conforms to or violates the established norms and values of a given society. Yet, the degree to which our survival depends upon receiving positive social and emotional responses in the form of acceptance has a disproportionate influence over our ability to succeed.

For example, if you are a highly skilled attorney working in a law firm, you may reasonably expect that your skills alone will allow you to win cases and earn the professional and social rewards you would expect. And in a normal environment in which emotional psychology operates as a social function that is subordinate to and responsive to professional performance, this would be the typical outcome. However, in an environment that may have been thrown out of balance by emotional predation and manipulation, professional performance alone may not be enough to win you the recognition and success you believe you have earned.

In fact, if the dynamics of interpersonal relationships are thrown out of balance significantly, professional performance and skill may be a secondary concern that has been made subordinate to your ability to achieve social acceptance and approval. And if the decisions about who receives social acceptance and approval are made by emotional predators, all of your professional skills and accomplishments may be regarded as a liability. So, an emotional predator can control you and hurt you by placing you in a position of inferiority and making you a captive audience in a social trap that you may not have the skills from which to extricate yourself.

Furthermore, social interactions and interrelationships are complex and difficult enough to manage in a natural setting. The contemporary environment is host to an entire complex apparatus of unprecedented developments in the form of social media, email, mobile phone technology, video conferencing, and other forms of electronic communication.

In his thesis "Emotion in Social Media," Dr. Galen Panger, a graduate of U.C. Berkeley's School of Information Management Systems, has identified certain parameters in his effort to determine whether the emotional psychology of social media users differs from the emotional psychology that characterizes people engaged in normal daily interactions.

According to his study, users of Facebook and Twitter did not display extreme or detrimental effects indicating that the social isolation caused by these new media has led to an increased development in antisocial personality disorder. However, he did establish that depending on the social media forum, users may tend to be more or less emotionally positive or negative. Specifically, Facebook posts were overwhelmingly characterized by positive emotional overtones, while Twitter posts tended to have a more negative tone.

Conversely, because Facebook posts tended to celebrate individual attributes in an emotionally positive and affirmative tone, Facebook users generally experienced more aggravation of negative emotions like jealousy and anger, while the negative town of Twitter posts worked to cure feelings of frustration and anger among users of the forum.

However, the study did not focus on one crucial element. The use of social media is itself an anomalous and unprecedented development in the evolution of human relationships and generally occurs when social media users are in social isolation. All true scientific studies must have a control group, but this study lacks one. The control group for any valid study of human psychology and emotion must be a natural environment devoid of technological interventions.

Although Dr. Panger's study established that there may be less variance or distortion among social media users when compared to each other, it uses environments largely regulated by technological communication as the default. The study does not address either how these disrupted environments compare to the human social and emotional psychology in non-technological environments, nor does it consider how technological communications devices and social media may enhance the ability of social and emotional predators to work in isolation, essentially unsupervised, to assemble profiles of their potential victims and create social personas that may strengthen their ability to succeed.

Thus, understanding the importance of emotional psychology and the presence of emotional predators is important for two fundamental reasons—our natural tendency is to seek social approval and acceptance, and our ability to succeed personally and professionally depends on maintaining an environment in which social rewards are distributed according to established norms. When this environment is skewed, whether in our own personal sphere of influence or in the larger professional or social environment in which we work or live, we lose the ability to fend for ourselves and sustain our own well-being. Upsetting this balance is precisely the goal of the social and emotional predator.

As a result, looking for signs of emotional and social manipulation in an effort to avoid such entanglements, and understanding how to respond and recover in the event we are caught off guard, are more than just refinement and sophistication; they are necessary skills for surviving and thriving in a world that has been dramatically altered and thrown off-balance in recent years.

# Tips for Reading and Analyzing People

### Overview: The Real Vampires

The most important step in recognizing the presence of a social or emotional predator is maintaining an awareness of the basic psychology of all emotional predators—whether they exhibit symptoms of psychopathy, Machiavellianism, or narcissism. Even if someone's behavior is not disruptive enough to be considered a sign of serious mental illness, anyone whose relationships depend upon their ability to emotionally manipulate others should be considered as potentially dangerous to your personal or professional safety and well-being.

It is important to take a moment to consider all of the material in the previous chapters and form a basic understanding of the psychology of a predator. This is because it is neither possible nor advisable to conduct a full-scale psychological analysis of everyone with whom you come into contact and because social and emotional predators' main skill set involves defeating efforts at detection.

All emotional predators share some common traits. As a result of some type of congenital psychological impairment at birth, as a result of some type of very serious emotionally or psychologically traumatic experience or series of experiences at a very young age, or as a result of some combination of these factors, emotional predators uniformly lack the ability to develop genuine emotional attachments with other people, to develop any deep, genuine feelings of warmth, to appreciate or value the feelings, thoughts, or rights of other people, or to develop any sense of respect for the principles and laws that govern society.

Furthermore, because these predatory individuals have learned from a very young age to live, survive, and even achieve high levels of success despite these serious psychological problems, they are unable to regard their condition as abnormal. They may regard their compromised psychological state as equal to or superior to a normal, healthy psychological state.

The second primary component common to all forms of predatory psychology follows from the first. Predators are unable to live like people who are not psychologically damaged. They are unable to form lasting, meaningful relationships, they are unable to find satisfaction in the daily routines and habits of life, and they are unable to see any value in the pursuit of traditional professional, personal, or academic goals.

Predators must live in a world that is not designed to serve their needs. As a result, the only feelings they are ever likely to develop toward so-called "normal" people are feelings of rage, jealousy, and hatred because they cannot ever have or do or experience the normal joy, happiness, and fulfillment that psychologically healthy people may take for granted.

Thus, when an emotional predator approaches you, there is a lot to consider. First, because predators have become very good at finding ways to live and hide their deficiencies, you may not realize that the person you are talking to is an emotional or social predator.

Second, people with healthy psychology can quite easily communicate with each other the reason they have made contact through basic conversation. However, a social or emotional predator cannot ever actually feel any genuine emotions and never really has any value for the goals and objectives you may consider important. They are always performing because they are not capable of living any other way. So, when predator begins a conversation with you, it may seem normal on the surface, but the motivations will also be devious and treacherous, and likely the only reason they have started a conversation is to establish trust and begin mining you for information.

Third, the goal of all predators is the same. You may likely regard your personal life and your professional career as your source of happiness and fulfillment, and your motivations may range from professional ambition to altruism and selflessness. But the predator can find happiness and fulfillment one way only—by destroying your happiness, your success, and even you. Because you have something the predator can never have, you are a constant reminder of his or her own damaged and compromised psychological makeup. Yet, predators, too, need to find some type of fulfillment and satisfaction, so they can relieve themselves of what would otherwise be an existence filled with unending boredom and pain.

Through a process of tortured and impaired evolution, the predator has learned to mimic your pursuit of happiness and fulfillment. However, because your avenues to success are off limits to predators, they have established a new route—controlling you in an effort to inflict pain, abuse, and damage on you. Thus, whereas you may feel guilt when you hurt someone, the predator feels joy and glee and relief. Your path to success is professional, academic, and personal accomplishment. The predator's path to success ids the destruction and abuse of others. Regardless of the specifics of how these character defects and psychological impairments manifest themselves, all emotional and social predators share the same basic psychological profile.

### *Early Signs That You Are Dealing with a Predator*

By now, we have examined the foundations of dark psychology, the psychological profiles that make up the Dark Triad, typical forms of manipulation in relationships, and how manipulation has manifested itself in society's institutions. This section provides guidance to help you understand when you may have come into contact with someone who is exhibiting signs of emotional or social predation.

First, remember that simply because you are not currently in a personal or professional relationship that could be defined as manipulative does not mean that you are free of all danger and concern. Predators have had to learn the hard way to live and achieve success using cold and calculating psychology from which they truly do not ever get any rest.

Imagine being injured in a serious accident and losing the use of one or more of your limbs—regardless of how much you would prefer to have the use of that limb back, you will be forced to find some way to adapt. Emotional predators do the same thing. But because their injuries are invisible, and because of the competitive nature of the business world, they sometimes hold an advantage over us if we fail to maintain vigilance.

Emotional predators can blend into the normal landscape because it is easy for them to go through the motions of daily living. They truly do not care if things don't work out because they have no value for their relationships or the things that society has established as having value.

Consider that the serial killer Ted Bundy worked on a crisis hotline while he stalked and murdered young women. He appeared successful, outgoing, handsome, and well-adjusted, but was not. Or consider that the serial killer John Wayne Gacy, who murdered and buried in the crawl space beneath his home almost 40 young men and boys, spent his days running a construction business, held fundraisers for local political leaders, and entertained sick children.

It may seem nauseating, especially with these extreme and dramatic examples, but for the emotional predator, important responsibilities in society are less a source of personal and professional satisfaction and fulfillment and more a perfect cover for their predatory addiction. As a result, you may find it helpful to develop some habits that will help you learn to identify some of the telltale signs of emotionally predatory behavior.

## Professional Relationships

- Be careful if you encounter someone who seems to use a lot of "props" or gimmicks when you initially meet them. For example, some people may have a habit of interposing their conversation with a so-called "winning smile." If this behavior seems to follow a pattern of repetitiveness or becomes excessive, it may be a warning sign.

- Other props and gimmicks may include a tendency to make lots of promises, a habit of presenting you with gifts, or "fast talk" like a sales pitch. This type of communication is often used to conceal an underlying lack of genuineness, with the predator relying on superficiality and material objects to prove his or her claims of affection.

- "If it seems too good to be true, it probably is." People use this as a reference to judge the relative honesty of business propositions every day. You can use the same frame of reference to detect whether you are dealing with an emotional predator. An emotional predator may often overcompensate for their inner emptiness and damaged psychology by creating an exterior image that is flawless to an unnatural degree.

- Emotional predators build self-esteem and value in their lives by destroying the self-esteem and value of the lives of others. One of their main tools is finding out what you like, what you value, and what you consider important so they can destroy it. Be cautious of people who seem to put in a lot of effort to win your confidence. They may do this in several ways:

  - Providing you with overwhelming support and encouragement.
  - Agreeing with all of your views and opinions.
  - Being very sweet, charming, and kind to a degree that you find out of the ordinary.
  - Offering you some type of intimate, personal secret to build trust. This is especially true if they pressure you to share something personal and intimate in return and react with anger if you refuse.
  - Sharing too much, too soon.

- All of us to some degree use some type of emotional influence in our relationships. There is nothing inherently wrong with relationships marked by a social dynamic; quite the opposite. However, if in your business dealings you encounter someone who displays the following tendencies to such a degree that they seem impossible to ignore, then use caution:

- ○ A sense of entitlement.
- ○ An attitude of superiority.
- ○ A tendency to dominate conversations.
- ○ An inflated ego.
- ○ A tendency to express jealousy.
- ○ An ultra-competitive perspective.
- ○ Hyper-critical comments.
- ○ Statements that seem to indicate that the person believes himself or herself to be beyond the reach of rules or laws or can only be understood by people of the highest rank.
- ○ People who play the blame game.
- ○ Double-dealing.

- "Grooming behavior" is a term usually used to describe the methods used by sexual predators. However, psychologists have agreed that emotional predators of all kinds use similar methods when they are preparing their victim for an attack. Especially with new acquaintances, watch for the following behavior patterns:

- ○ A period of befriending and gaining the trust of the victim.

- Befriending and gaining the trust of the victim's associates.
- Looking for opportunities to be alone with the victim.
- Giving gifts or money to the victim.
- Talking about inappropriate subject matter that may be intimate, overly personal, or involve illegal activity, and trying to make it sound normal or even fun, often in an effort to desensitize the victim to such language.
- Attempts to make physical contact.
- Personal comments about appearance or other forms of flattery.
- Being unusually kind, generous, and helpful.
- Assessing behavior, such as asking about your habits and routines.
- Opening efforts to exert control and influence, such as secrecy, blame, and even threats.
- Strategic efforts to create private encounters in which you are a captive audience.

If you suspect that someone in your professional environment is engaging you in these predatory activities, ask yourself the following questions:

- Do you feel isolated from friends and family?

- Have your values changed?

- Do you feel guilty or afraid to express yourself?

## *Personal Relationships*

While all of these behaviors may be present in the workplace, especially among people you don't know personally and in an environment that rewards ultra-competitiveness and ruthlessness, your pursuit of personal relationships may also be plagued by an abundance of emotional predators. Although the psychology and motivation are the same, the tactics may be quite different. Some of the common technique's predators will use in social situations are listed below:

- The need for control is a common element that can lead to the end of a relationship:
    - Excessive contact in an effort to establish your dependency on their approval.
    - Unhealthy or aggressive responses to rejection in an effort to impose limits and boundaries.
    - Endless debating and negotiating.
    - Physical aggression.

- Poor treatment of other people.
- Unexplained demonstrations of anger

- A demonstrable need to provoke:
  - Debasing comments.
  - Overuse of sarcasm.
  - Attempts to create feelings of jealousy.
  - The silent treatment

- Inconsistent behavior:
  - Projection and gaslighting.
  - Superficial charm.
  - Frequent disappearances and absences.
  - Attitude changes.
  - Intermittent reinforcement.

### *Professional or Personal Relationships*

Not everyone's life is perfectly organized or compartmentalized. Often environments and the people in them cross boundaries. Often in our daily lives, we wonder where things may have gone wrong. Quite often the answer may be that we are trapped in a relationship with an emotional predator.

Regardless of the environment in which you meet people, you should always maintain a vigilant lookout for any of the following telltale signs of a predatory personality:

- People who are pathologically selfish. They may go through the motions of friendship and love, but their emptiness is apparent when they fail to initiate social outings or when all encounters leave you feeling exhausted and drained.

- Emotional predators may offer lots of charm and flattery, but if there is a lack of substance to your interactions with them, you can be sure the compliments are probably false, too.

- Predators will exaggerate their accomplishments, and even lie. If you call them on it, they will refuse to take responsibility or admit that they are wrong.

- A date or outing with an emotional predator may always be a high-stakes adventure. If you never seem able to engage with them simply over a cup of coffee and have a happy and fulfilling encounter, you may be dealing with a predator.

- Predators are bullies by nature and use anger as their primary means of communication. Avoid people who demonstrate a tendency to humiliate people or challenge anyone who seems to have more power or success than they do. Predators also use insults and putdowns to build themselves up. You may notice this kind of conduct directed at other people when you are out with a predator. For example, if you are at a café or restaurant a predator may try to impress you by insulting or humiliating the staff.

- Predators are manipulative, which they often show by making promises and then not keeping them.

- Because predators lack a conscience and do not understand that their abusive behavior should make them feel bad, a telltale sign may be anyone who boasts about committing abusive actions or crimes.

- Predators may also display parasitic behavior. If you are involved with someone who is excessively lazy and uses you, you should find a way to end the relationship.

# Practical Tips for Dealing with Predators

Of course, identifying the signs of predatory behavior is only half the battle. The other half is finding a way to resolve the conflicts and repair the damage that inevitably follow in the wake of an encounter with an emotional predator.

Following are some general guidelines. Some of the tips are meant as suggestions that you should implement on a daily basis. They should become new habits that will now be part of your daily routine. It is important not to regard these tips as chores or burdensome or a diversion or interruption of your normal life. Think of these suggestions as your own personal investment in your daily professional development.

If a virtuoso musician who plays violin for a symphony wants to stay at the top of his profession, then no matter what else he does, one thing must remain constant: daily practice and a constant effort to stretch his repertoire by seeking out more challenging pieces, finding new forms of expression, and adding new skills to his resume. Or, consider a university professor in any department—being hired into a tenured position is the only beginning. The "publish or perish" mentality will soon take hold, and he will find that continually refreshing his professional assessment of his area of expertise is as much a part of his daily professional routine as the more mundane tasks involved in classroom lectures.

So it is with life in the modern world. To maintain a position of success and happiness and fulfillment, we must think like any gifted performer or professional. Constant vigilance and the continual addition of new weapons to your arsenal to fight the war against the growing threat of epidemic levels of emotional predation will keep your calendar full.

Buy a notebook, start a new spreadsheet, create a new folder in your favorite browser's bookmarks tab, and clear off a shelf on the bookcase in your office. This effort in your life can be just as much a passion and an investment in your own success and happiness as the money you spent earning your college degree or the time and effort you spent building your professional network.

Most importantly, as we move down the list of tips for dealing with predators, remember that it is not unusual to find that recovery from such encounters, in some cases, may take years. Though the first step of dealing with a predator is ensuring they are no longer physically present in your life, this step is not always easy to accomplish. And once you achieve this goal, actually repairing the damage they have caused may keep you very busy for some time to come. But relax—though the damage inflicted by emotional predators can grow increasingly worse over time, so the benefits of successfully dealing with these incursions can have increasingly beneficial returns over time.

Here are some suggestions:

- **Conduct a self-inventory**: From time to time, review the section in Chapter 3 that details the types of character traits that make people more susceptible to emotional predation. Look within and be honest with yourself about your weaknesses. Don't do this as an exercise in self-abuse, though.

  Consider that an emotional predator approaches you with only one goal in mind—to destroy you. You may not be entirely willing to examine yourself in an unflattering light, but an emotional predator who has made you a target may not have time for anything else.

- **Be cautious:** Whenever you are meeting new people, whether romantically or professionally, guard your personal information.

- **Resist projection and gaslighting**: When you encounter these environments, remind yourself that the goal is to defeat all genuine efforts to establish accountability.

- **Keep a journal**: You don't have to be creepy about it, but respect yourself enough to take your personal and professional aspirations seriously. Write down your thoughts and concerns at the end of the day, even if you can only manage a few sentences. The blank page will never pose the kind of threat to you that an emotional predator may.

  By getting your complicated thoughts out of your head and on paper, you have unburdened yourself in a way that is most beneficial to you. A predator knows you have this need, and their willingness to listen may be designed as a trap.

- **Go "no contact"**: If you are in a professional or personal relationship and notice any of the signs of emotional predation, take steps immediately to end the relationship. Sometimes that may mean not replying to text messages, voice mail messages, or email messages. The predator may not like it and may react angrily, but if you try to enter into a negotiation or debate, you will be playing into their hands. Just state simply that you have decided not to respond any further, then stick to your plan.

  This is called going "no contact," and in the modern world with all its digital communication, it is a valid and acceptable tactic. If the predator continues to harass you, keep notes and document their abuse. You may need to use it later if law enforcement becomes involved. Screenshots, text messages, email messages, and voice mail messages should all be saved and kept in a folder.

- **Get help:** Recognizing that you are in a relationship with a predator is the first step to escaping the relationship. Rescuing yourself must become your first priority. Remember that you will require professional help to solve this problem. If you are unsure how to proceed, take ten minutes out of your day, find a quiet place and make a phone call. Don't worry about being perfect or feeling awkward, professionals expect you to be at a loss and will know how to help.

- **Find a support network:** You may need to seek the support of the law enforcement authorities. If you believe things are that bad, you are probably right. Don't allow yourself to be bullied or intimidated. As with a call to a psychologist or helpline, making the first call is the most important step. Even if things don't go exactly the way you think they should, by informing the local authorities, you will have placed yourself in a better position

- **Reinvent yourself:** Remember that as a victim of emotional predation, you will no longer be the person you once were and will have to restructure your thoughts and approaches to life.

- **Cheer up:** You have taken the first step toward defeating the predatory influences that have brought the dark cloud over your life. This is the first day of the rest of your life, not the last day of the life you used to live.

As you move forward with your new awareness of the nature of your surroundings, the world may become a less intimidating place, and you will once again find the joy and happiness that seems to have been missing for so long.

# Conclusion

Many of us, if not all of us, have been involved in a relationship with an emotional predator at one time or another.

Whether you recall a particularly bad dating experience in which your partner seemed to treat you with an absolute disregard for your thoughts and feelings. Whether you have been employed at a company that continually seems unwilling or unable to recognize your contributions. Whether you have been among the few of us who have had a close encounter with an emotional predator and suffered real physical harm, you know now that dark psychology is a force to be reckoned with.

Now that you have read this book, you have a solid foundation for formulating an effective and lasting strategy that can help you understand when someone is trying to exploit you. Moreover, now that you understand the mindset shared by all predators, you will be less likely to be victimized in the future.

As you move forward, remember that the study of dark psychology has a legitimate foundation in clinical psychology. Remember also that not all forms of social influence are necessarily bad, and that many of the programs of self-development currently available in the professional marketplace can help you develop your psychology in healthy and productive ways that can help you succeed.

I hope that by reading this book, you have encountered some basic truths about the nature of the relationships that surround you. I also hope that you will use this new knowledge to formulate a plan of action, so you can once again take control of your life and leave behind the burden of emotional manipulation once and for all.

*Brandon Goleman*

# References

14 Signs of Psychological and Emotional Manipulation. (n.d.). Retrieved from https://www.psychologytoday.com/us/blog/communication-success/201510/14-signs-psychological-and-emotional-manipulation

3 Signs of an Inconspicuous Predator in Your Midst. (n.d.). Retrieved from https://www.psychologytoday.com/us/blog/shadow-boxing/201406/3-signs-inconspicuous-predator-in-your-midst

4 Signs of A Machiavellian Personality Disorder. (2018, August 27). Retrieved from https://www.spring.org.uk/2018/08/machiavellian-personality-disorder.php

Abrams, B. S. L. (2018, September 29). Are you being emotionally manipulated? Retrieved from https://www.ebony.com/love-relationships/are-you-being-emotionally-manipulated/

Barnes, S., & Barnes, S. (n.d.). 9 signs you're being emotionally manipulated by your significant other. Retrieved from https://hellogiggles.com/love-sex/9-signs-youre-emotionally-manipulated-significant-other/

Boissoneault, L. (2017, May 22). The true story of brainwashing and how it shaped America. Retrieved from https://www.smithsonianmag.com/history/true-story-brainwashing-and-how-it-shaped-america-180963400/

Brainwashing. (n.d.). Retrieved from https://www.merriam-webster.com/dictionary/brainwashing

Brainwashing. (2019, September 14). Retrieved from https://en.wikipedia.org/wiki/Brainwashing

Britannica, T. E. of E. (n.d.). Brainwashing. Retrieved from https://www.britannica.com/topic/brainwashing

Brown, J. (2018, July 12). This is how normal life feels as a psychopath. Retrieved from https://medium.com/s/story/this-is-how-normal-life-feels-as-a-psychopath-2294c3f36311

Brown, L. (2019, August 24). 10 disturbing signs of emotional manipulation that most people miss. Retrieved from https://ideapod.com/signs-emotional-manipulation/

Byrne, T. (2015, October 15). Beware of the emotional predator. Retrieved from https://goodmenproject.com/featured-content/beware-of-the-emotional-predator-dg/

Cherry, K. (2019, July 15). 5 myths about hypnosis debunked. Retrieved from https://www.verywellmind.com/what-is-hypnosis-2795921

Clarke, J. (2019, April 12). How to recognize someone with covert narcissism. Retrieved from https://www.verywellmind.com/understanding-the-covert-narcissist-4584587

Cohut, M. (2017, September 1). Hypnosis: What is it, and does it work? Retrieved from https://www.medicalnewstoday.com/articles/319251.php

Comparison of light triad to dark triad. (n.d.). [Online image]. Retrieved from https://www.frontiersin.org/files/Articles/438704/fpsyg-10-00467-HTML/image_m/fpsyg-10-00467-t006.jpg

Covert Conversational Hypnosis Webinar. (n.d.). Retrieved from https://www.transformdestiny.com/hypnosis/covert-conversational-hypnosis-home-study.asp

Covert Hypnosis. (n.d.). Retrieved from https://www.the-secret-of-mindpower-and-nlp.com/Covert-hypnosis.html

Dilts, R. B. (1999). What is NLP? Retrieved September 30, 2019, from http://www.nlpu.com/NLPU_WhatIsNLP.html

Effect of emotional intelligence on job performance. (n.d.). [Online image] Retrieved from https://www.researchgate.net/profile/Daniel_Newman9/publication/41087511/figure/fig3/AS:668543704125448@1536404648453/Cascading-model-of-emotional-intelligence-EI-The-cascading-model-is-based-on-the.png

Emotional Intelligence (EQ): The Premier Provider - Tests, Training, Certification, and Coaching. (n.d.). Retrieved from https://www.talentsmart.com/articles/9-Signs-Youre-Dealing-With-an-Emotional-Manipulator-2147446691-p-1.html

Emotional Predators. (n.d.). Retrieved from https://psychopathyawareness.wordpress.com/tag/emotional-predators/

Experts Say These 7 Common Phrases Are Actually Emotional Manipulation. (n.d.). Retrieved from https://www.bustle.com/p/what-does-emotional-manipulation-look-like-7-lines-people-may-use-to-control-others-to-be-aware-of-18175851

Get the Life You Want Starting NOW! (2010, April 4). Retrieved from https://www.nlppower.com/

Holland, K. (2018, February 13). How to recognize the signs of emotional manipulation and what to do. Retrieved September 30, 2019, from https://www.healthline.com/health/mental-health/emotional-manipulation

How To Recognize The 8 Signs Of Emotional Manipulation. (2019, August 5). Retrieved from https://liveboldandbloom.com/02/relationships/emotional-manipulation

How to Spot Common Predator Characteristics. (2018, January 22). Retrieved from https://www.sterlingvolunteers.com/blog/2018/01/spot-common-predator-characteristics/

Hypnosis. (n.d.). Retrieved October 1, 2019, from
https://www.apa.org/topics/hypnosis/

Hypnosis. (n.d.). Retrieved from
https://www.psychologytoday.com/us/basics/hypnosis

Hypnosis. (2019, September 20). Retrieved from
https://en.wikipedia.org/wiki/Hypnosis.

Hypnotherapy - Hypnosis. (n.d.). Retrieved from
https://www.webmd.com/mental-health/mental-health-
hypnotherapy#1

Kandola, A. (n.d.). Neuro-linguistic programming (NLP): Does it
work? Retrieved from
https://www.medicalnewstoday.com/articles/320368.php

Kassel, G. (n.d.). 11 signs you're dating a narcissist — And how to get
out. Retrieved September 30, 2019, from
https://www.healthline.com/health/mental-health/am-i-
dating-a-narcissist#15

Khazan, O. (2014, March 1). The dark psychology of being a good
comedian. Retrieved from
https://www.theatlantic.com/health/archive/2014/02/the-
dark-psychology-of-being-a-good-comedian/284104/

La Fayette, Marie-Madeleine Pioche de La Vergne de. (1780). *La
Princesse de Cleves*. Paris.

Layton, J. (2019, May 1). How brainwashing works. Retrieved from
https://science.howstuffworks.com/life/inside-the-
mind/human-brain/brainwashing.htm

Leary, M. R. (2015, December). Emotional responses to interpersonal
rejection. Retrieved from
https://www.ncbi.nlm.nih.gov/pmc/articles/PMC4734881/

Machiavelli, Niccolò. (2004). *The Prince*. London: Penguin.

Machiavellianism. (2019, September 24). Retrieved from
https://en.wikipedia.org/wiki/Machiavellianism

McLarty, B.D. (2015). [Online image]. The devil at work: Understanding the dark side of personality and its impact on performance. Retrieved from https://www.semanticscholar.org/paper/The-Devil-at-Work%3A-Understanding-the-Dark-Side-of-McLarty/52d642007166340842ec2c3ba15e91672e941fb6

Meet the Machiavellians. (n.d.). Retrieved from https://www.psychologytoday.com/us/blog/machiavellians-gulling-the-rubes/201509/meet-the-machiavellians

Melley, T. (2011). Brain warfare: The covert sphere, terrorism, and the legacy of the cold War. *Grey Room*, (45), 19–40. Retrieved from https://www.jstor.org/stable/41342501?read-now=1&seq=1#page_scan_tab_contents

Model of hypnosis. (n.d.). [Online image]. Retrieved from https://tedmoreno.com/2014/09/10/hypnosis-101-what-is-hypnosis/

Moore, R. (2018, September 19). The brainwashing myth. Retrieved from http://theconversation.com/the-brainwashing-myth-99272

Morris, G., & Morris, G. (n.d.). Behavioral indicators of antisocial personality disorder. Retrieved from https://www.activebeat.com/your-health/6-behavioral-indicators-of-antisocial-personality-disorder/?utm_medium=cpc&utm_source=google&utm_campaign=AB_GGL_US_MOBI-SearchMarketing_TR&utm_content=s_c_303621126873&cus_widget=&utm_term=psychological&cus_teaser=kwd-10865291&utm_acid=3040947159&utm_caid=1599827680&utm_agid=63349425987&utm_os=&gclid=EAIaIQobChMIhLfKyKrn5AIVA4TIChovbgW_EAAYAiAAEgJlXfD_BwE

Narcissism. (n.d.). Retrieved from https://www.psychologytoday.com/us/basics/narcissism

Narcissism. (2019, September 27). Retrieved from https://en.wikipedia.org/wiki/Narcissism

Narcissistic Personality Disorder. (n.d.). Retrieved from https://www.psychologytoday.com/us/conditions/narcissistic-personality-disorder

Narcissistic Personality Disorder. (2017, November 18). Retrieved from https://www.mayoclinic.org/diseases-conditions/narcissistic-personality-disorder/symptoms-causes/syc-20366662

Narcissistic Personality Disorder. (2019, July 12). Retrieved from https://www.helpguide.org/articles/mental-disorders/narcissistic-personality-disorder.htm

Nedelman, M. (2018, February 13). Are you susceptible to brainwashing? Retrieved from https://www.cnn.com/2018/02/13/health/brainwashing-mind-control-patty-hearst/index.html.

Neuro-Linguistic Programming (NLP). (n.d.) Retrieved from https://www.skillsyouneed.com/ps/nlp.html

Neuro-Linguistic Programming Therapy. (n.d.). Retrieved from https://www.psychologytoday.com/us/therapy-types/neuro-linguistic-programming-therapy

NLP model of therapeutic change. [Online image]. (n.d.). Retrieved from https://i.pinimg.com/originals/20/67/07/206707645d0afe5d59610322d25b920a.jpg

NLP Training Courses & Neuro-Linguistic Programming Techniques. (n.d.). Retrieved from http://www.thenlpcompany.com/

Nuccitelli, M. (2006). Dark psychology - Dark side of human consciousness concept. Retrieved from https://www.ipredator.co/dark-psychology/

Nuccitelli, M. (2006). Dark psychology - Dark side of human consciousness definition. (n.d.). Retrieved from https://www.darkpsychology.co/dark-psychology/

Nuccitelli, M. (2019). Dark psychology - Definition of the psychological construct. Retrieved from https://www.darkpsychology.co/dark-psychology-definition/

Panger, G. T. (2017). *Emotion in Social Media* [Dissertation].

Platform. (n.d.). Retrieved from https://www.alegion.com/solution/platform?utm_source=ad words&utm_medium=ppc&utm_term=nlp neuro linguistic&utm_campaign=NLP&hsa_net=adwords&hsa_ver =3&hsa_ad=356028543502&hsa_src=s&hsa_cam=2038305 254&hsa_acc=1622984630&hsa_kw=nlp neuro linguistic&hsa_tgt=kwd-310275137465&hsa_grp=70406593365&hsa_mt=p&gclid=E AIaIQobChMIycjyvp_s5AIVsCCtBh2JAA_NEAAYAyAAEgl8z PD_BwE

Plinkleton. (2015, October 10). Study finds some psychopaths have enhanced recognition of others' emotions. Retrieved from https://www.psypost.org/2015/08/study-finds-some-psychopaths-have-enhanced-recognition-of-others-emotions-37116

Predation. (2019, September 29). Retrieved from https://en.wikipedia.org/wiki/Predation

Psychological Manipulation. (2019, September 20). Retrieved from https://en.wikipedia.org/wiki/Psychological_manipulation

Psychopathy. (n.d.). Retrieved from https://www.sciencedirect.com/topics/medicine-and-dentistry/psychopathy

Psychopathy. (n.d.). Retrieved from https://www.psychologytoday.com/us/basics/psychopathy

Psychopathy: A Misunderstood Personality Disorder. (n.d.). Retrieved from https://www.psychologicalscience.org/news/releases/psycho pathy-a-misunderstood-personality-disorder.html

R Blair, R. J. (2013, June). Psychopathy: cognitive and neural dysfunction. Retrieved from https://www.ncbi.nlm.nih.gov/pmc/articles/PMC3811089/

Ramey, S. (2017, January 23). How to escape the cage built by an emotional predator. Retrieved from https://exploringyourmind.com/escape-cage-built-emotional-predator/

Recognize Emotional Predator Traits and Behaviors. (2019, July 23). Retrieved from https://emotionalpredators.com/recognize-emotional-predator-traits-and-behaviors/

Resnick, B. (2017, March 7). The dark psychology of dehumanization, explained. Retrieved from https://www.vox.com/science-and-health/2017/3/7/14456154/dehumanization-psychology-explained

Rossner, J. (2014). *Looking for Mr. Goodbar*. New York: Simon and Schuster Paperbacks.

Selfcarehaven. (2018, May 12). Dating emotional predators: Signs to look out for. Retrieved from https://selfcarehaven.wordpress.com/2014/08/29/dating-emotional-predators-signs-to-look-out-for/

Signs and Traits of Narcissists, Crazymakers, Emotional Manipulators, Unsafe People. (n.d.). Retrieved from http://thinklikeablackbelt.com/blog/signs-and-traits-of-emotional-predators/

Storytel AB. (n.d.). Dark psychology: Learn to influence anyone using mind control, manipulation and deception with secret techniques of dark persuasion, undetected mind control, mind games, hypnotism and brainwashing. Retrieved from https://www.storytel.com/se/sv/books/638795-Dark-Psychology-Learn-To-Influence-Anyone-Using-Mind-Control-Manipulation-And-Deception-With-Secret-Techniques-Of-Dark-Persuasion-Undetected-Mind-Control-Mind-Games-Hypnotism-And-Brainwashing

Taylor, B. (2018, October 8). Machiavellianism, cognition, and emotion: Understanding how the Machiavellian thinks, feels, and thrives. Retrieved from https://psychcentral.com/lib/machiavellianism-cognition-and-emotion-understanding-how-the-machiavellian-thinks-feels-and-thrives/

Team, G. T. E. (2018, December 2). Neuro-linguistic programming (NLP). Retrieved from https://www.goodtherapy.org/learn-about-therapy/types/neuro-linguistic-programming

The 30 Most Disturbing Human Experiments in History. (n.d.). Retrieved from https://www.bestpsychologydegrees.com/30-most-disturbing-human-experiments-in-history/

The Art of Brainwashing. (n.d.). Retrieved from https://www.psychologytoday.com/us/blog/brain-chemistry/201803/the-art-brainwashing

The Human Predator—Spot and Deal With Them—Open Minds Foundation. (2018, April 5). Retrieved from https://www.openmindsfoundation.org/faces_of_undue_influence/what-is-manipulation/human-predator/

The Stealthiest Predator. (n.d.). Retrieved from https://www.psychologytoday.com/us/articles/201805/the-stealthiest-predator

Therapy, H. (2019, August 31). What is Machiavellianism in psychology? Retrieved from https://www.harleytherapy.co.uk/counselling/machiavellianism-psychology.htm

Watching out for Emotional Predators. Are You Being Brainwashed into Becoming a Manipulation or Emotional Abuse Victim? (2019, June 13). Retrieved from https://loveandabuse.com/watching-out-for-emotional-predators-are-you-being-brainwashed-into-becoming-a-manipulation-or-emotional-abuse-victim/

What is Neuro-Linguistic Programming - NLP - and Why Learn It? (2019, September 14). Retrieved from https://inlpcenter.org/what-is-neuro-linguistic-programming-nlp/

What is NLP? (n.d.). Retrieved from http://www.nlp.com/what-is-nlp/

Note:

Made in the USA
Coppell, TX
11 February 2020

15716830R00098